About Island Press

Since 1984, the nonprofit organization Island Press has been stimulating, shaping, and communicating ideas that are essential for solving environmental problems worldwide. With more than 1,000 titles in print and some 30 new releases each year, we are the nation's leading publisher on environmental issues. We identify innovative thinkers and emerging trends in the environmental field. We work with world-renowned experts and authors to develop cross-disciplinary solutions to environmental challenges.

Island Press designs and executes educational campaigns in conjunction with our authors to communicate their critical messages in print, in person, and online using the latest technologies, innovative programs, and the media. Our goal is to reach targeted audiences—scientists, policymakers, environmental advocates, urban planners, the media, and concerned citizens— with information that can be used to create the framework for long-term ecological health and human well-being.

Island Press gratefully acknowledges major support of our work by The Agua Fund, The Andrew W. Mellon Foundation, The Bobolink Foundation, The Curtis and Edith Munson Foundation, Forrest C. and Frances H. Lattner Foundation, The JPB Foundation, The Kresge Foundation, The Oram Foundation, Inc., The Overbrook Foundation, The S.D. Bechtel, Jr. Foundation, The Summit Charitable Foundation, Inc., and many other generous supporters.

The opinions expressed in this book are those of the author(s) and do not necessarily reflect the views of our supporters.

THE
SPIRIT OF
DIALOGUE

THE
SPIRIT OF
DIALOGUE

Lessons from Faith Traditions in
Transforming Conflict

Aaron T. Wolf

Washington | Covelo | London

ISLAND PRESS is a trademark of the Center for Resource Economics.

Keywords: mediation, dispute resolution, negotiation, arbitration, intractable conflicts

Library of Congress Control Number: 2017940668

All Island Press books are printed on environmentally responsible materials.

Manufactured in the United States of America
10 9 8 7 6 5 4 3 2 1

*This book is dedicated with love and
appreciation to my parents, Leonard and Deborah,
who first guided me along the path,
and who walk with me still.*

Contents

Preface

This book is designed to be a practical guide for anyone who is involved in leading or participating in difficult conversations, which, if we are honest, is most of us. Whether we are professional facilitators or simply trying to improve relations with our loved ones and those around us, the conflicts with which we all deal take place within ourselves, between individuals, in small groups, and between nations, and they happen in our families, at work, and at the negotiating table.

In the West, we are generally trained to base our approach to managing conflicts on rationality: "People will agree when it's in their interest to agree." Tools typically focus on what is measurable and quantifiable. We "separate the people from the problem" and "insist on objective criteria." If only we could see the tangible benefits of cooperating, we are taught, we simply would.

Over my 20 years as a facilitator and scholar working through and studying conflicts over shared water resources around the world, I have come to appreciate both the limitations of the rational models on which we in the West base our understandings of conflict and cooperation and the wisdom, constructs, and practical tools of the world's faith traditions in working toward deep and healthy interactions around contentious issues. I've spent 2 years traveling the world and 8 intervening and subsequent years of reading and discussing these questions with practitioners from a variety of the world's faith traditions and with those who have negotiated conflicts in a breadth of settings.

This book describes what I found and how to use it.

It draws from the worlds of rationality and of spirituality to offer an approach for managing and transforming conflict at all levels, from the intrapersonal to the international. It includes personal reflections on successes and setbacks encountered in negotiations and trainings around the world, and it is bolstered throughout with skills-building exercises for readers to enhance their own capabilities for conflict transformation in their own lives.

Professionals who lead meetings or facilitate small groups will benefit, of course, as will government officials and diplomats, because their training probably did not include many of the powerful approaches and tools that are covered here. In addition, as an academic, I tried to make sure the book has enough academic rigor to be included in university coursework related to conflict resolution and environmental issues, with enough U.S. and international examples to be relevant to both.

Given the breadth of potential applications, I tried to keep the tone practical and accessible but not light or superficial. It is designed to provide frameworks to work from and tools to work with, regardless of whether the process is official or not. Because the book is for both those who lead and those who participate, I include skills-building exercises throughout, but they are not intended solely for facilitators or mediators. Shaping the conversation comes just as powerfully from skillful participation as it does from whoever is nominally steering the process.

A note on limitations:

Serious scholars or practitioners of religion may be disappointed or even appalled at the generalizations or mischaracterizations I make here. I know enough from my own tradition to understand how much I am conflating when I write things like, "In Buddhism, the practice is . . . ," or, "Muslim thinking suggests. . . ." I do know that adherents of each tradition have widely divergent beliefs and practices depending on geography, school, lineage, and, sometimes, individual teacher. I am probably inconsistent in theologic structures and transliteration style—for example, I know I move from Sanskrit to Pali terms, depending on the source—and I'm pretty confident that a number of things I say are limited or flat-out wrong.

For all this, I am truly and deeply sorry.

Despite these limitations, not least of which is the time it takes to grapple with the nuance of even the one tradition in which I was raised, I forge ahead, hopeful that what this book is really about are the tools and structures that are used to inform better dynamics. It is these tools that matter here, more than the nuance of their roots. I do try to provide enough source material so that those so moved will be able to dig deeper and to discover the power and beauty of the teachings in their own contexts.

Acknowledgments

In the 13 years it's taken me to go from being a Western-trained scientist and mediator to being able to pull something like this work together, I've been blessed to be helped along the way by a vast number of kind and generous souls.

First and foremost, I'd like to thank Oregon State University as an institution, and particularly my academic home in the College of Earth, Ocean, and Atmospheric Sciences (CEOAS). As one might imagine, the experience of writing a book such as this from a college of science at a public, land-grant university could have gone a lot of different ways. To my great pleasure (and occasional surprise), I have received nothing but support and encouragement from my students, colleagues, and administrators, for which I am deeply grateful. The Center for the Humanities kindly gave fellowship support for this work, and the professionals at CEOAS's Research Publishing and Outreach Office were first rate, especially Abby Metzger, the office director, who was invaluable in helping to shape the entirety of the work, and David Reinert, who crafted the beautifully drawn figures. Caryn Davis of Cascadia Editing spun her usual magic on the text and images, for which I am always grateful, and Cassandra Hatcher stepped in at a critical juncture.

Most of those who took the time to teach me from their profession, faith, or both are mentioned in the body of the text, where the reader will get more context, and I am more grateful than I can say to each. I was extremely fortunate to be able to spend time with Professor Ramón Llamas and his sponsors at the Botin Foundation, who led an effort pulling ethics, faith, and water together; and Professors Eran Feitelson and Suwit Laohasiriwong, who hosted me so generously in Israel and Thailand, respectively. I am extremely grateful to those who took the time to teach me along the way, whether individually or in their workshops and trainings, especially Mustafa Abu-Rabia, Vahid Alavian, Robert Beatty, Reb Ozer Bergman, Jerry Delli Priscoli, Erica Ariel Fox, Prof. Father José Galván,

Sheikh Fara Gaye, Peter Gleick, Marc Gopin, Rhea Graham, Elias Jabbour, Edy Kaufman, Michelle LeBaron, Albert Lincoln, Barbarah Miller, Leonard Riskin, Marshall Rosenberg, Shaiya Rothberg, Jay Rothman, Santikaro, Yona Shamir, Swami Subodhananda, Narayanan Vasudha, Phra Paisan Visalo, Rabbi Uzi Weingarten, Ya'qub ibn Yusuf, and Muhammed Zaki.

People were likewise incredibly generous with their artwork and exercises, including Badege Bishaw, Caryn M. Davis, Sean P. Davis, Terrence E. Davis, Martin Fowler, Paul Heussenstamm, Orit Martin, Carolyn Myss, Ariella Wolf, and the Columbia River Inter-Tribal Fish Commission.

A number of friends and colleagues were kind enough to read early drafts of the text and offer helpful comments, including Vahid Alavian, Rabbi Benjamin Barnett, Tara Bennett-Goleman, Lynette de Silva, Daniel Goleman, Glen Hearns, Dena Marshall, Kim Ogren, Michele Ribeiro, Subbappa Ribeiro, Ariella Wolf, and Deborah Wolf.

At Island Press, my editor, Emily Turner, has been incredibly generous and supportive throughout a long and meandering process. I am grateful too to Sharis Simonian, production editor and answerer of *many* last-minute queries; Carol Anne Peschke, crazy-good copy editor; and Jaime Jennings, publicity maven.

As ever, nothing I do or am is possible without the support and love of Ariella, my lovely wife, and Yardena and Eitan, offspring extraordinaire.

CHAPTER ONE

The Boundaries of Science?

A Tale of Two Vaticans

There are two Vatican Cities, one public and one private. The former many know and have experienced, perhaps swept in a crowd through the Vatican Museums, hushed gently by the guards while trying to take in the power and nuance of the ceiling of the Sistine Chapel—or through the pope's weekly homilies, offered to the thousands who gather in St. Peter's Basilica and Square most Sundays and Wednesdays.

The entrance to the other, private Vatican has been famously shielded for the past 500 years by the Papal Swiss Guards, instantly recognizable in their tri-color Renaissance uniforms and 7-foot halberds. Attempt to pass and you will be politely but firmly rebuffed.

Unless you can prove you belong.

For example, if you are a guest of St. Martha's Hostel, you flash your brass key ring adorned with the papal crest, and the guard comes to attention, salutes, and allows you to pass. Instantly, the hum of the crowds melts away as you enter through a narrow passageway into an entirely different Vatican City.

St. Martha's is an unimposing modern building just south of St. Peter's Basilica, constructed in 1996 by Pope John Paul II primarily to house the College of Cardinals when they congregate to elect a new pope. John Paul II had participated in two conclaves himself, and he commissioned the construction to make the process more comfortable and less strenuous on the mostly elderly cardinals.

Figure 1.1. *Pope Francis enters Domus Sanctae Marthae (by Pufui Pc Pifpef I [CC BY-SA 3.0], via Wikimedia Commons from Wikimedia Commons).*

In intervening years, however, the hostel is used to house those with formal business with the church (and has been retrofitted to include the residence of the retired Pope Benedict). One will not find large-screen TVs or broadband Wi-Fi in the rooms, and the only decoration is a small wooden cross above the bed. But the service, mostly by nuns, is impeccable; the international cuisine (including kosher and halal) is spectacular, and the sheets are the softest you will ever experience. Seriously, you won't want to get out of bed.

I got access to this Vatican City because of water conflicts.

In 2004, the Program in Water Conflict Management and Transformation at Oregon State University, which I direct, was supported by the Carnegie Corporation to co-sponsor a series of meetings with Peter Gleick's Pacific Institute on cutting-edge issues related to water resources that are shared, often contentiously, across international boundaries. Peter, one of the world's foremost thinkers in the water policy arena, and I decided that a series of dialogues between professions that don't necessarily interact but who might learn from each other could be useful. One meeting, for example, was held at Sandia National Laboratories between people who managed water internationally and those in the security world responsible for monitoring arms control agreements. Both work in worlds where suspicion is rife and data are scarce, and both have access to different technologies and institutions they try to use to overcome both the suspicion and the lack of data.

I had the idea, for reasons I'll go into in a bit, to similarly bring together the worlds of international water resources and spiritual transformation. Peter had the idea to bring in one of the few institutions in the world whose mandate could be construed to include both water science and spirit: the Pontifical Academy of Sciences.

Let's stipulate at this point that the Catholic Church has had some, well, issues with science over the years. Galileo comes to mind.

Many will therefore be surprised to learn that the current position of the Catholic Church is that if church doctrine and scientific knowledge are in conflict, it is church doctrine that must change. And it is the Pontifical Academy of Sciences that monitors the potential tensions between the two.

Better yet, and with more immediacy for the story at hand, participants and organizers of meetings co-hosted by the Pontifical Academy are housed in St. Martha's Hostel, beyond the saluting Swiss Guard, on the quiet side of Vatican City.

The actual 3-day meeting was . . . challenging. We had twenty-six participants from all over the world, a mix of water professionals who had negotiated international agreements at a very high level and leaders from a variety of faith traditions who had thought, taught, or written about the process of spiritual transformation. Finding a common language, or even a common framework, in our short time proved difficult. On one hand, a former water minister from Nepal described the importance of dialogue in monitoring biochemical oxygen demand, while the Sufi mystic next to him said little but smiled so brightly and practically glowed with positive energy that you just wanted to sit next to him in hope that some might rub off on you. A water professional from the Middle East stormed out because someone used the term "battle of civilizations" in a way he found offensive (the meeting was held during the second year of the second Gulf War), while a bishop, a representative of the Pontifical Academy, shook his head in his hands and muttered, "This isn't science."

So although the group came up with few answers for whether there is overlap between the worlds of water negotiations and spiritual transformation,[1] a couple of key questions did emerge, questions that became the focus of my research life for the next 12 years, questions that have implications for conflict transformation far beyond the world of water, questions that are at the heart of this book:

- How are anger and conflict explained within the world of spiritual transformation, and how can that understanding be applied to conflict management?

- What tools and techniques are invoked to enhance personal or group transformation within these settings and might be reflected in other situations?

I've spent 12 years traveling the world when I could, reading and discussing these questions in intervening periods, both with practitioners from a variety of the world's faith traditions and with those who have negotiated conflicts in a breadth of settings. I've studied Kabbalah in Jerusalem, sat with a Buddhist monk who mediates forestry disputes from his temple in northern Thailand, and worked from an ashram in India with a rural development organization started by a Hindu swami. I've had the good fortune to meet with facilitators who work from Catholic, Protestant, Jewish, and Muslim perspectives, to learn that mediation processes are explicitly described in the central texts of both the Quaker and Bahá'í faiths, and to have read and explored the energy work around anger and conflict of native cultures in the Americas and elsewhere.

This book describes what I found and how to use it.

But first, some background.

How a Water Scientist Hit the Limits of His Worldview—Twice

The meeting in Vatican City, and for that matter this book, came about because of a seminal conversation I had had a year earlier with a friend now serving in the Secretariat of the World Governing Body of the Bahá'í Faith in Haifa, Israel. In his earlier incarnation, he had been the senior water advisor at the World Bank. (*Incarnation* in this instance is meant figuratively. I know I need to specify in a book like this; I was once at a New Age-y dialogue training and was asked to turn to the person next to me and describe one of the most difficult conflicts I'd ever been involved with. I started with, "Well, in another life I was a soldier. . . ." At which point my young partner interrupted with, "That's so cool! In another life, *I* was a princess!")

In 2003, the year before the Vatican meeting, I was a member of a panel addressing problems particular to international waters at the World Bank's Water Week in Washington, D.C. At that time, I was 6 years into practicing as a facilitator and mediator of problems created by conflicting interests over water resources that cross the boundaries of countries or economic sectors, while a professor in the Department of Geosciences at Oregon State University.

Basically, water management *is* conflict management. There is always too little clean, reliable water for everyone's needs, resulting in seemingly perpetual disputes between, at one level, farmers, indigenous groups, environmentalists, urban users, and industrialists and, at another, between nations that share waterways. As someone trained in the sciences, I had approached the problems scientifically, collecting data about shared waterways, including developing the largest collection of water treaties in the world and compiling other factors related to both conflict and cooperation. Our Program in Water Conflict Management and Transformation became a one-stop shop for disputed waters, where one could map out the likely trends and triggers of conflicts while designing processes for monitoring and resolving them or, better, preventing them from breaking out at all.

In fact, I had begun my career focusing solely on the scientific aspect of water, concentrating on groundwater and modeling its flow. Having grown up in northern California, punctuated with several years in Israel, I understood that water resources underlie some of the more intractable political issues of our times, and I had set out on a path to learn to help resolve these issues, using water as the language.

But the only water language I knew was technical. Surely if people had the right data, they would come together in harmony. Or so I thought.

My first jolt out of complacency with the science as *the* answer to politics came ironically as I began my career as a scientist years earlier, in the late 1980s. With a master's degree focusing on groundwater, I was working for the U.S. Geological Survey in Wisconsin as a water scientist in my first attempts to solve real-world problems.

Pretty Lake, Wisconsin is, in fact, quite a pretty lake in the rural southern part of the state, about an hour west of Milwaukee. But its level was dropping, and the people who lived along its banks were concerned about their views and their docks. Our mathematical models suggested that the drop in lake level was probably caused by a nearby farmer's increased pumping of his well for irrigation; the well tapped the groundwater that fed the lake.

Triumphant in our science, we held a meeting with the property owners to share our findings. The first problem we encountered was that most landowners simply weren't buying it. One suggested that he was sure recent dredging had "broken the plug" in the bottom of the lake, not a theory grounded in hydrology. Others asked whether we were 100 percent

Figure 1.2. *Near Pretty Lake, Wisconsin (© 1978 Terrence E. Davis. Used with permission).*

certain of our findings. Like responsible scientists, of course we weren't. The final problem came when someone asked what the solution was. At the time in Wisconsin, there was no legal connection between groundwater and lake water, despite a clear hydrologic connection, and the farmer could not be legally obligated to do anything at all for the property owners. The only solution was for them to talk through their differences and see whether they could find a mutually agreeable way forward.

As scientists, our job was done. And profoundly unsatisfying.

This was the beginning of my gentle dawning that simply having the "right" answers was not enough to bring people together; people had their ideas of how the world works, and no amount of data was necessarily going to change their minds. Moreover, it was clear that people are at the heart of *all* of these issues—they cause the problems and must likewise craft the solutions—and I had no training in people whatsoever.

It was around then, as I was grappling with these gaps in my education, that an officemate back from an internship in Washington, D.C. first mentioned the term *environmental conflict resolution,* a concept I'd never heard of but one that instantly resonated. Surely people are just systems like any other, but perhaps with greater uncertainties. And I was fine with uncertainties. (Groundwater science is rife with uncertainty. In another task, I had spent 3 months calculating that a plume of pesticides flowing underground toward a nearby municipal well would reach the well at some point between 5 and 50,000 years from then. Again, the results were deeply unsatisfying to the constituents who needed to figure out what to do about the problem.) Learn about the human system, combine it with understanding of the natural system, and the solutions would be unassailable.

That jolt—that people are actually at the center of both conflicts and resolution—sent me back to school for a Ph.D. focusing on policy analysis and conflict resolution.

Like most training in the United States at the time in what has become known as alternative dispute resolution (ADR), mine was based primarily on the work coming out of Harvard's Program on Negotiation. The seminal text that had essentially launched the field in the modern United States was Fisher and Ury's 1981 classic *Getting to Yes*, still an excellent introduction to the field. That and subsequent work by Fisher and Ury, both together and separately, spawned a pantheonic library of work offering alternatives to the costly, all-or-nothing approach of the U.S. legal system.

The *alternative* in ADR puts people at the center of the process and urges resolution to issues in which everyone gains something: *mutual gains bargaining, win–win solutions*, and *integrative approaches* are all terms from the field that suggest the benefits of ADR over the legal process, in which the setting is overtly confrontational and one party wins everything and the other nothing.

Getting to Yes essentially suggests a four-part process to dispute resolution:

- Separate the people from the problem.
- Focus on interests, not positions.
- Invent options for mutual gain.
- Insist on using objective criteria.

This approach generated a quantum leap forward at the time, especially in the countries of the developed West, particularly the United States, in which there really seemed so few alternatives to law. And fortunately for someone with a scientific background, the approach, human-centric as it was, was blessedly rational. "Separating," "focusing," "inventing," and "objectivity" are all musical concepts to the scientific mind. In fact, entire subfields were spawned in which disputes were reduced to their mathematical cores, with interests, benefits, and objective criteria all quantified and modeled, so that the mutual gains could be determined numerically.

"Alternative" though it was, ADR fit my rational worldview perfectly. And then I started to practice.

Again, ADR was a huge leap for me, and it was profoundly useful as I gently moved into the worlds of mediation and facilitation around water conflicts at a variety of scales, from farmers and environmentalists in the western United States to representatives of countries that shared waterways that crossed their international borders. Initially, I was invited to meetings of stakeholders to present research on the settings that are more or less conducive to conflicts over water resources, then I was increasingly asked to chair maybe a session or two, until finally I was helping to facilitate and eventually designing processes, including leading the facilitation or mediation on my own.

And that combination of research-based and applied work with stakeholders in water disputes got me invited to be on a panel on water at the World Bank's Water Week in 2003.

During my talk, I put up two figures of river systems (figure 1.3).

The maps come from an exercise that Len Abrams at the World Bank had designed for coursework on resolving disputes over waterways shared by two or more countries, and I use the pair regularly in my own work. The map on the left shows the way most people think about their rivers, if they think about them at all. Shown are all the boundaries—the lines that separate us—between nations, states, economic sectors, and ethnic groups. In the map on the right, the way water professionals tend to see the world, the only delineation is of the watershed itself. Everything within this container is connected to everything else: surface water and groundwater, quality and quantity, and all the humans and ecosystems that reside within. I used these images to suggest that our job in water conflict management is to balance the views expressed in each, learning

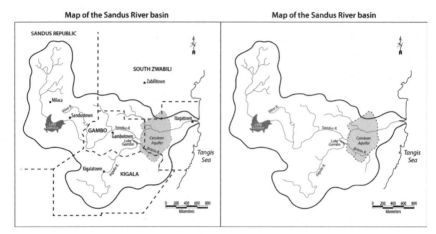

Figure 1.3. *Map of the fictitious Sandus River basin, with and without boundaries.*

to manage the water system as if the only boundaries were hydrological, focusing on what unites us while still respecting the very real needs expressed through political boundaries: sovereignties, economic systems, and community cohesion.

At a break in the meetings, I was musing with Vahid Alavian, a good friend and mentor at the World Bank, about the sudden ripple of energy that seemed to emanate throughout a room of stakeholders whenever I showed them a map of their own watershed without the political boundaries. It always felt initially disorienting ("Where am I on the map, and where are the issues I am here to represent?") but then gently transforming ("Oh, I get it, we really are all connected."). The discussions invariably took on a slightly warmer hue as we proceeded from this exercise.

Vahid was the senior water advisor at the World Bank at the time, having come from years at the Tennessee Valley Authority. He had also been instrumental in bolstering the World Bank's educational capacity at the World Bank Institute, so he was coming with decades of experience in water resources development, training, and group process. What I did not know about him at the time, probably for reasons I'll get into in the next chapter, is that Vahid also has a deep spiritual life as a practicing Bahá'í (and until recently served in the Secretariat of the faith at their World Centre in Haifa).

BOX 1.1

EXERCISE

See if you can find a map of the watershed in which you live, ideally one that does not show political boundaries. If you are in the United States, the term for the unit is *watershed*, and the U.S. Geological Survey is a good place to start (http://nhd.usgs.gov/wbd.html). If you are in a British-English speaking country, the term is *catchment*, and you might start with the World Resources Institute (http://www.wri.org/publication/watersheds-of-the-world) or your own national geologic survey.

Once you find the map, notice what you notice. Do you instinctively look for your home town? Try to identify where state or province boundaries would lie? Now try to broaden your view: Does the map evoke thoughts of any new relationships? Is the process disorienting or comforting?

I remarked that it often seemed that advances with stakeholders came in sporadic moments of transformation, flashes when suddenly everyone in the room seemed to see something differently than a moment before or abruptly understood something new about the problem or the path forward. These moments felt very similar to the wave of energy I felt when people saw their boundaryless water basin for the first time.

Vahid's experiences were similar, and our conversation moved from why we thought this particular pair of images was so powerful to thinking about where one learns more about transformative moments, especially if they seem so crucial to the process of working through tense situations.

We considered other instances of these sudden shifts in understanding. Certainly, in life cycle events, one experiences them fairly regularly. Becoming a parent for the first time, for instance, drastically shifts one's worldview, often in a matter of minutes. One moment you are the center of your own universe, the next you are holding a helpless bundle of needs for which you are obviously responsible, who is clearly screaming to you, "Really? I don't care a whit about your accomplishments and degrees. Feed me!"

Or, God forbid, when someone gets sick, often again resulting in an immediate shift where people vow to eat more healthfully, exercise more, and spend more time with their loved ones.

Yet where does one learn about transformation in a way that would be useful in conflict settings? Certainly one shouldn't suggest parenthood or heart attacks as homework. And certainly not in any of the mediation coursework I knew about at that time.[2]

As Vahid and I continued to play with the two maps and the importance of the transformative moment in conflict settings, he made a suggestion that altered the course of my life:

Vahid proposed that an analog for the transformative moments we'd seen in tense negotiations might be found in the world of spiritual transcendence.

"After all, don't these two maps represent what faith traditions have been urging for millennia? That we stop looking at the world through our boundaries and immediate wants? But rather see the world as through the map on the right, through connections and relationships, to our family, our communities, and to the divine? Why don't you explore the process of spiritual transformation in faith traditions of the world," he suggested, "to see what you might bring into the mediation world?"

Initially, all the little red flags in my head went up. As a scientist and rationalist in a public, land-grant institution, I had always worked within the premise that anything faith related was private, and it certainly should not inform one's research. And as a member of a minority faith in the United States, I had innate suspicion of anyone talking publicly about religious issues; more often than not, they wanted to condemn my practice or pitch an alternative.

But good science goes where the evidence leads, regardless of perceived societal boundaries; to do otherwise would be disingenuous. And, precisely because I am a rationalist and a utilitarian, I could not shake the fact that the suggestion made eminent sense, simply too much sense to ignore.

Fortunately, I had tenure (in a college of science at a state university, no less), so I could not get fired for asking the question. (And actually I don't think I would have been regardless. All of my colleagues and administrators have been very supportive of this work.)

I also had a sabbatical coming up, which allowed me the time and freedom to pursue the answers. And Peter Gleick at the Pacific Institute and

I had just received support from the Carnegie Corporation for a series of meetings pairing the worlds of water conflict with other seemingly unrelated issues to see what one might learn at their intersect.

"Water negotiations and spiritual transformation?" I suggested.

"Vatican City?" he offered.

And here we are.

CHAPTER TWO

Healing the Enlightenment Rift

*In the Western world it is widely held that only positivistic
reason and the forms of philosophy based on it are universally
valid. Yet the world's profoundly religious cultures see this
exclusion of the divine from the universality of reason as an
attack on their most profound convictions. A reason which is
deaf to the divine and which relegates religion into the realm
of subcultures is incapable of entering into the dialogue of
cultures.*

Pope Benedict XVI, The Regensburg Lecture, 2006

The Nile River basin is one of the most complex in the world, both
hydrologically and geopolitically. It is a vast basin—more than 3 million square kilometers, about the size of India—inhabited by 238 million
people in eleven countries. Almost all of the water originates in Ethiopia
and in the countries of the Equatorial Lakes; as it flows northward to the
delta, the climate becomes increasingly arid until the river finally termi-
nates in Egypt, where there is almost no rainfall at all.

For decades, there has been (and still is, for all intents and purposes)
a longstanding deadlock between upstream nations and downstream
Egypt. Many of the upstream nations have only recently begun to develop
their water resources, especially large irrigation and hydropower projects.
In contrast, for Egypt, which has relied on a relatively undiminished flow
of the Nile since time immemorial, upstream dam building is immensely
threatening to what it considers its lifeblood. Hydropolitical relations have

Figure 2.1. *Night observation of the Nile River (by NASA/Scott Kelly [Public domain], via Wikimedia Commons from Wikimedia Commons).*

ebbed and flowed over the years, with sporadic negotiations and institutional advances punctuated by tension and even occasional talk of war.

Relatively speaking, 2006 was a good year. A Nile Basin Initiative had been established a few years earlier, under which the countries were working hard to develop mechanisms for dialogue to help ease tensions between upstream and down. In October of that year, I had the chance to offer a "Water as a Tool for Peace" workshop with country representatives in Entebbe, Uganda, at a meeting sponsored by the eleven nations of the initiative.

The meeting began with country presentations and, as often happens in dialogue over international basins, each side focused on their rights and what they thought they deserved. Upstream users insisted on their rights to develop irrigation and hydropower dams, and downstream riparians focused on their historic rights to the river's unchanged flows. Many in the international community, mostly representatives of development banks and European aid agencies, have tried to shift these discussions away from rights and strict allocations to instead focus on sharing the benefits that

Figure 2.2. *Fishermen on the White Nile, Uganda (by Bernard DuPont from France [CC BY-SA 2.0, desaturated from the original], via Wikimedia Commons from Wikimedia Commons).*

water brings, whether through hydropower, flood control, or irrigation. The idea is that each water use has tangible benefits and costs, usually expressed in dollars (the power generated or waste produced, for example). On paper, the benefits of cooperating for region-wide development far outweigh the costs, and the hope among some in the development world was that awareness of these potential benefits would overwhelm the political risks of cooperating.

As a World Bank economist finished a presentation on how to quantify these benefits and share them equitably, a young Ugandan woman from a local environmental nongovernment organization raised her hand.

"Just so I understand this situation correctly," she began, "this was not an 'international basin' until you all drew your nice straight lines across our continent from the comfort of some bureaucratic office in Berlin more than one hundred years ago. Then, because it's now 'international,' it falls under some new law that we also had no voice in crafting, and to figure out how to cooperate under this new law, we need to use your values and measures to figure out what is important to us so that we can share it, ignoring many of the central issues on which we base our relationship with the river—respect, honor, community, spirituality. Do I have that about right?"

Although the economist glossed over the implications of her question, the point was clear: Discussions over such seemingly objective and quantifiable concepts as "benefits" are based on worldviews, and the two exhibited in this dialogue clashed profoundly. Both the World Bank presentation and the young woman's question are emblematic of what I call the Enlightenment Rift, understanding of which can help bridge the gap between such apparently disparate perspectives.

The Enlightenment Rift and Its Legacy: How Deciding to Sever the Worlds of Rationality and Spirituality 300 Years Ago Leaves Us Ill Prepared to Transform Complex Problems

The concept that the worlds of rationality and spirituality are separate and distinct is a relatively recent phenomenon, common only in very specific places in the world, a product of eighteenth-century Western Europe. Although the perspective may be recent and localized, its legacy in our modern approach to problem solving is profound and spreading, particularly in the developed North. What we now call the Enlightenment, carried out as new advances in science paralleled extreme excesses in European church politics, resulted in a conscious severance of the worlds of rationality and spirituality, with intense implications for today's clash of ideas. In temporal terms, it suggested that day-to-day considerations should be gauged in measurable, "objective" concepts, whereas the world's spiritual dimension should be considered separately, in the evening at home or within one's Friday, Saturday, or Sunday community.[1] Over time, "rationality" dictated the structure of subsequent paradigms, from economics to science to modernity. Today, we in the North are consistently satisfied to ask the "what" without the "why," at least in public discourse. We talk comfortably of economic growth rates, for example, without the accompanying discussion of what simply creating and owning more stuff does to our soul. We are able to put the emphasis in debates over crime disproportionately on the value of punishment and retribution and regularly less on the potential for the individual and his or her community for rehabilitation and reconciliation.[2] We regularly turn to benefit–cost analyses as a decision-making tool, where all factors must be reduced to economic value, explicitly excluding profound but intangible elements.

In his famous and powerful Regensburg Lecture of 2006, Pope Benedict XVI gave a moving history of Catholic theology's inherent inclusion of both rationality and spirituality: "In the beginning was *logos*, and *logos* was with God, and *logos* was God."[3] This balance has been challenged from Hellenic times through Kant (who famously said that he needed to set thinking aside in order to make room for faith), modernity, and now postmodernity.[4]

Similarly, most elucidations of Buddhism have corresponding depictions: "Dhamma is, literally, 'that which supports': it is the Truth within us. . . . In Dhamma there is no creed and there are no dogmas. . . . This is because faith in a Buddhist sense is not a blind quality but is combined with wisdom."[5]

Thus, the idea of separating out rationality from spirituality is a fundamentally recent, fundamentally Western construct. As Huston Smith, one of the premier scholars of the world's religions, eloquently puts it, "The modern West is the first society to view the physical world as a closed system,"[6] whereas much of the thinking in the global South and East often retains its integration of rationality and spirituality.

As models, consider figure 2.3, which shows frameworks from two different spiritual traditions that illustrate the idealized relationship between self and community, between justice and mercy, and between boundaries and expanse. Figure 2.3a models three of the ten Kabbalistic *sefirot*, or emanations of divine attributes.[7] These three show a balance between *din*, the attribute of justice,[8] boundaries, and self, with the *sefirah* of *chesed*, the attribute of lovingkindness, concern for the other, mercy. Within this tradition, one attribute cannot exist without the other, and the two remain in exquisite balance—but not quite. In this equilibrium of divine attributes, the *sefirah* of *chesed*, lovingkindness, is always modeled just a touch higher, connoting that that attribute takes precedence in any conflict between the two. (Any parent understands this construct intuitively. Raise a child with

Balance in Conflict

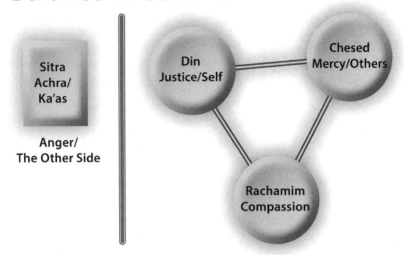

Figure 2.3. *Modeling balance in conflict:* (a-above) *shows three of the ten Kabbalistic* sefirot, *or emanations of divine attributes;* (b-left) *the balance of self and other, light and dark, can be seen in the* Taijitu, *the traditional Taoist symbol for* Yin *and* Yang *(figures by David Reinert, Oregon State University, 2016).*

justice alone, and the result will be an unfeeling bully. Raise him or her with only lovingkindness, and the child will become unbearably spoiled and self-centered. And, truth be told, whenever we're conflicted between which of the two approaches to take with our loved ones, we generally can't help but favor mercy.)

As the map of the *sefirot* shows, the balance of *din* (justice) with *chesed* (mercy) is manifested in the *sefirah* of *rachamim* (compassion). The attribute of *rachamim* is very explicit in what is meant by *compassion*, suggesting a precise integration of consideration for both justice and mercy, for self and community, for boundaries and expanse. The root of *rachamim* is the same as for *rehem*, womb, giving us a very clear allusion to what is meant: A mother is able to give not only nourishment but her very life force to her unborn child (ultimate lovingkindness) but is able to do so *only* if she takes care of her own health and needs.

The message of the construct has relevance for many of the grand issues of the day. Do we pursue justice or mercy in our lives and politics? Shall we be concerned with individual rights or responsibility to one's community? Modernity or postmodernity? Free market or safety nets? Right or left? Red or blue? The answer given by this understanding to all these choices is, "Yes, in exquisite balance." The dichotomies are false, as is the apparent division between rationality and spirituality.

This balanced construct exists fairly universally and can influence approaches to resource allocation, negotiations, and understanding of relationships. Many traditions have an understanding of a balance between justice and mercy (or self and other, profane and holy, or, for that matter, rationality and spirituality), often coming together in a third attribute, referred to as compassion: empathizing with the other while being true to oneself. For an anatomic visualization of this trinity, picture if you will the two sides of our brain: the systematic, planning left side and the more expansive, present right side, coming together in the emotional center of our heart.

The unity of a balance of self and other, light and dark, can be seen in the *Taijitu*, the traditional Taoist symbol for yin and yang (figure 2.3b), where the nondual whole is understood as the dividing line between the two dissipates. In Hinduism, these attributes are similarly recognized in the face of the god Shiva when portrayed as the Trilocana, or *Tryambaka Deva*—literally, the Three-Eyed Lord. The Sun (symbolizing love) is his right eye, the Moon (symbolizing justice) is the left, and fire is the third. Symbolically the third eye of wisdom, balancing the attributes of the other two, is perceptive and capable of destroying evil (see figure 2.4). In Christianity, the same relationship can be understood in the Holy Trinity: Father, the Hebrew Bible god of laws; Son, New Testament manifestation of absolute lovingkindness; and Holy Spirit, which balances the two throughout the world at large. Some Christian Kabbalists make these comparisons explicit, although naturally understandings of each are much

Figure 2.4. *An artistic representation of Shiva and the 12 Jyotirlingas associated with him (by Ved Sutra [http://vedsutra.com/media] [CC BY-SA 4.0], via Wikimedia Commons from Wikimedia Commons).*

more nuanced.[9] In Islam, *Al-Hakam*, the Judge, *Ar-Rahman*, the Merciful, and *Ar-Rahim*, the Compassionate, are the three common names of the ninety-nine names of Allah, and Abou El Fadl[10] describes Islamic processes for "institutionalizing mercy and compassion in social interaction."

In the foundational documents describing the Bahá'í faith's House of Justice, this balance is reinforced: "Nothing short of the spirit of a true Bahá'í can hope to reconcile the principles of mercy and justice, of freedom and submission, of the sanctity of the right of the individual and of self-surrender, of vigilance, discretion and prudence on the one hand, and fellowship, candor, and courage on the other."[11]

(In 1994, John Nash won the Nobel Prize for his work, which contradicted the traditional view that economics is driven solely by individuals pursuing their own rational self-interest, in favor of his "Nash equilib-

rium," the meeting point where individual interests are balanced by the
needs of the group. Apparently science does eventually catch up.)[12]

One sees the tri-poled balance in historic architecture throughout Buddhist, Hindu, and Confucianist Asia. Temples often have three doors: The
general population enters on the left, the side of compassion, and comes
out on the right, the side of enlightenment. Only monks go through the
middle door. Similarly, palaces have three doors: Soldiers use the left,
scholars the right, and only the king uses the middle.[13]

So, to generalize, the heavy (over)emphasis on rationality and the
rights of the individual over the inclusion of spirit and the needs of the
community is disproportionately a Northern and Western phenomenon,
associated primarily with the non-Asian, post-Enlightenment, developed
world. The global South and East often retain a more integrated view
of issues of the individual with the community or one's spirituality with
one's rationality, as do indigenous communities around the world. These

Figure 2.5. *Confucius Temple, Taipei City, Taiwan (by Udo Schoene [Own work]
[CC BY-SA 3.0, desaturated from the original], via Wikimedia Commons from
Wikimedia Commons).*

two profoundly contradictory worldviews—the North/West's dichoto-
mous views of rationality and spirituality, justice, and mercy, in stark contrast to the South/East's holistic, integrated balance—clash regularly and
intensely across the world stage, from foreign policies to expectations of
immigrant communities to dynamics in the United Nations. In other fora,
one might even note the global implications this geography has on the
current "clash of civilizations,"[14] and it is central to how we communicate
across scales and boundaries.

The Enlightenment Rift and the Transformation of Disputes

Similarly, in what has become known as alternative dispute resolution
(ADR), common approaches stress the rational. As discussed in the previous chapter, in Fisher and Ury's 1981 classic *Getting to Yes*, probably still the
most influential book in the field, the authors suggest that we "separate
the people from the problem" and "insist on objective criteria." If only we
could see the tangible benefits of cooperating, we are taught, we simply
would.

Yet, as noted above, this reductionist viewpoint prevails in only a very
small part of the population of the world—primarily Europe and North
America—and is incredibly recent at that. Throughout human history,
the sciences were about understanding divine creation, and it was clearly
understood that what was measurable was only a small portion of human experience, and usually not the important part at that. Deifying the
quantifiable, and accepting only what is measurable as fact, places undue
blinders on our understanding of the world and creates a conundrum of
the undiscovered: Did things we are only now learning to measure not
exist beforehand? Were the nonvisible spectrum of light and subatomic
particles articles of faith until we learned to gauge them? Did meditation
create less empathy before scientists measured how the brain physically
changes with regular practice? And if not, why do we discount all that we
cannot measure simply because we have not yet learned how?

Likewise in mediation, for so much of the world, the concept of
"separating the people from the problem" simply makes no sense at all.
Although rational facilitation can help allocate scarcity in a way that is
quantifiable, it says little about the values that are paramount for so much

of the world: honor, community, face, spirit. People *are* the problem. But they are also the solution, especially if we work with them holistically, from both sides of our brain, the rational *and* the transcendent.

To be fair, the field now known as ADR came about precisely because of the limitations and cost of the Western legal framework. But as exemplified by Fisher and Ury and its offshoots, ADR is more often than not rooted in both rationality and economic constructs of interests and benefits. Some practitioners claim that ADR works because the mediator can help parties construct agreements that meet the needs of the parties: People agree when it is in their interest to agree. Well, how does one know it was in the parties' interests to agree? The only proof is tautological: They agreed.

But *are* negotiations rational? Do we agree only when it is in our interest to agree? Or is something more going on in the room, especially when there is even a modicum of real emotion present, something connected more to energy and transformation? Successful multiparty negotiations require profound transformations in the way participants engage with the issues at hand. Those involved can often point to the precise moment when thinking altered dramatically—the "aha!" moment—where emphasis shifted from individuals thinking only of their own agenda to also understanding the needs of others. As noted above, traditional conflict resolution models define these moments in rational terms: "People come to agreement when it is in their interest to agree." Even overlooking the tautological nature of this argument, "rationality" often does not hold sway if the conflict involves even a modicum of real emotion.

To really understand the process of transformation, and the settings most conducive to inducing these shifts, it may be beneficial to look outside the field of conflict resolution as defined in modern, academic terms. As noted in the previous chapter, when one thinks of the settings most conducive to transformative thinking, the world of spiritual transformation rises as potentially the most appropriate. Every spiritual tradition in the world, after all, is devoted to precisely this process of transformation: to aid individuals in moving from a focus on their own immediate wants and desires to addressing their obligations and connections to society, humanity, and the divine.

The focus here is what spiritual *processes* of transformation can offer the world of negotiations and conflict management. Thus, the scope of each individual application is by necessity smaller—small groups of stakeholders at best—yet the overall potential to effect change in thinking about the process of conflict management is vast.

Manfred Halpern (1924–2001), professor emeritus of politics at Princeton University, developed his theory of transformation as the root of both personal and political change, based largely on Sufi understandings, as applied to international relations. He wrote, "Transformation is a process of participating in creation so that we may give birth to something fundamentally new that is also fundamentally better."[15]

Very little work has explicitly tied spiritual transformation to conflict negotiations and management, although what has been done suggests exciting potential. In February 2003, the Program on Negotiation at Harvard Law School launched The Harvard Negotiation Insight Initiative, specifically to offer mediators and stakeholders resources to "explore the interface of contemporary negotiation theory and practice with alternative frameworks including some drawn from perennial wisdom traditions."[16] Although the initial focus was in the realm of legal mediation in the United States, the first workshop, held in June 2004, brought a variety of facilitators and mediators together for training, including a handful with environmental expertise. As the annual workshops have grown, the focus has broadened to all branches of mediation and negotiation. Nonetheless, much of this activity focuses on the spirituality of the mediator, an important but separate issue, and material that does draw from spiritual traditions is often secularized for palatability in the West.

My sense, in contrast, is that we can learn much by making the roots of these teachings explicit and by offering them from the context in which each was developed. I've found that it is worth naming the sources from which these collected tools and approaches are drawn and talking explicitly not only about why it is so difficult in the Western context to do so but also about how that blind spot hinders our ability to truly transform conflict.

Literature does exist on the potential for applying the tools of spiritual and ethical process to conflict transformation, suggesting potential applications to environmental issues as well. Transformative mediation, a relatively new branch of ADR, offers an alternative to "problem-solving" mediation (which can be highly directive and focused on short-term problem solving), based on "empowerment and mutual recognition of the parties involved" and on their long-term interests.[17] "Compassionate listening" is a faith-based technique of guided communication that has proven to be effective in extremely hostile settings, notably by Carol Hwoschinsky in guiding dialogue between Israelis and Palestinians who have experienced violence.[18] Rabbi Uzi Weingarten teaches similar techniques of "communicating with compassion," which have been applied in a variety of hostile settings.[19] Abou El Fadl[20] describes Islamic processes for "institutionalizing mercy and compassion in social interaction," McConnell[21] structures mediation in a Buddhist construct, and Barthel[22] suggests lessons for process from a Bahá'í perspective.

The Association for Conflict Resolution (ACR) now has a Spirituality Section, and the fall 2005 issue of its journal, *ACResolution*, focused on "Spirituality and the Heart of Conflict Resolution." Although most of that activity focuses on the mediator's own spirituality,[23,24] or on mediation as a spiritual practice,[25] some work does draw directly from the spiritual world to facilitate the process of conflict resolution.[26]

Marc Gopin,[27] director of the Center for World Religions, Diplomacy and Conflict Resolution at George Mason University, suggests at the potential for conflict resolution to learn from spiritual transformation:

> One example [of the possibilities of merging study of religion and conflict resolution] is the spiritual process of transformation of character through reflection and ethical improvement of one's behavior. Several theories of conflict resolution suggest the importance of personal transformation for the resolution of deep conflicts. Spiritual programs of personal transformation might be combined with this kind of conflict resolution methodology in religious settings. . . . Could such phenomena be incorporated into conflict resolution strategies among religious peoples or even more generally?

BOX 2.1

SOURCES FOR FURTHER READING

Several practitioners in the United States have written articles encouraging the use of spiritual tools in facilitation settings, especially Eileen Barker, Daniel Bowling, Kenneth Cloke, Carol Hwoschinsky, Joanna Macy, and Leonard Riskin. But as far as I can find, there are no books for a general audience that explicitly draw on the tools and frameworks of the spiritual world and offer them in the context in which they were developed. There are several that do draw from one or two traditions but that largely secularize the text for the Western audience. Among the best are these:

Erica Ariel Fox, *Winning from Within: A Breakthrough Method for Leading, Living, and Lasting Change* (New York: Harper Business, 2013).
Marc Gopin, *Healing the Heart of Conflict: Eight Crucial Steps to Making Peace with Yourself and Others* (Kutztown, PA: Rodale Books, 2004).
Michelle LeBaron, *Bridging Troubled Waters: Conflict Resolution from the Heart* (San Francisco: Jossey-Bass, 2002).
John Paul Lederach, *Building Peace: Sustainable Reconciliation in Divided Societies* (Washington, DC: U.S. Institute of Peace, 1997).

Another literature that touches on these issues consists of books written within one faith tradition and geared toward members of that faith. Among those, the most noteworthy are these:

Jennifer E. Beer and Eileen Stief. *The Mediator's Handbook* (Gabriola Island, BC: New Society Publishers, 1997; Developed by the [Quaker] Friends Conflict Resolution Programs).
Elias Jabbour, *Sulha: Palestinian Traditional Peacemaking Process.* (Montreat, NC: House of Hope Publications, 1993, 1996).
Mohamed M. Keshavjee, *Islam, Sharia & Alternative Dispute Resolution.* (London: I.B. Tauris, 2013).
John A. McConnell, *Mindful Mediation: A Handbook for Buddhist Peacemakers* (Bangkok, Thailand: Buddhist Research Institute, 1995).
Ken Sande, *The Peacemaker: A Biblical Guide to Resolving Personal Conflict,* Third Edition (Grand Rapids, MI: Baker Books, 2003).
Carolyn Schronck-Shenk, ed., *Mediation and Facilitation Training Manual, Fourth Edition* (Akron, PA: Mennonite Conciliation Service, 2000).

And of course just about anything by Thich Nhat Hanh. I have found this especially useful:

Thich Nhat Hanh, *Transformation & Healing: Sutra on the Four Establishments of Mindfulness* (Berkeley, CA: Parallax Press, 1990).

None of these texts, in either category, are written specifically with an environmental focus.

Isn't Religion at the Heart of Most Conflicts? What Faith Traditions Can Teach about Transformation

In the late 1990s, as I became increasingly active as a facilitator, I also became progressively interested in how water conflicts are resolved in indigenous cultures. Although most of my work at that time was around international waters, it seemed logical that there would be tools and techniques in those settings where tribal or village water conflicts must have broken out and been resolved for millennia. In 1997, I had the chance to spend some time with both the Berbers of the Atlas Mountains in North Africa and the Bedouin of the Negev Desert in Israel to learn from their leaders about their methods for resolving their disputes.[28]

The time in the Atlas was very productive, but when I started asking about past conflicts among the Bedouin, I hit a wall. "No, we've never had a conflict over water," I was told repeatedly. How was that possible, I wondered: five permanent wells, thirty major tribal groups, archeological evidence of redoubts where soldiers must have guarded their tribe while watering at the well. No conflicts, ever?

Finally, in one tent in a small *wadi* in the Negev Desert, just north of a huge new Israeli airbase at Avdat, a younger man who was listening to my questions with his grandfather, started to reflect on one conflict between two tribes that he had heard of. As he began to tell me about the tensions and how they had escalated, his grandfather stormed out the room, clearly upset.

"What's up?" I asked.

"Well, after the dispute, the tribes had done *sulha*, a ceremony of forgiveness. And after the ceremony we consider the dispute never to have happened; it is essentially erased from history."

"He seems pretty upset; this must have been fairly recent, yes?" "Yeah, fairly recently. I think it happened around 350 years ago."

∼

In the years since I started speaking publicly, often in academic settings in the West, about reuniting the worlds of science and transcendence in conflict transformation, someone invariably asks, "Isn't religion at the

Figure 2.6. *In the Atlas Mountains. The author with Hammou Magdoul (left), a farmer in Ameskar el-Fouqani, and interpreter Mohamed Zaki (right) (photo courtesy of the author).*

heart of most conflicts? What can they possibly teach about transforming conflict?"

First, let's distinguish between religion and spirituality.[29] The latter loosely involves the recognition of some universal connection, however that may be understood, occasionally glimpsed through moments (or longer) of transcendence, however that may be experienced.[30] For the strict atheist, the connection might simply be understood through Einstein's recognition that the entire universe is made up either of energy or of potential energy (matter). In some nondual understandings, that is carried one step further: Just as matter and energy are simply different forms of the same entity, so are energy and consciousness and, therefore, the entire universe is made up of either consciousness or potential consciousness. How we experience the transcendent moments that lead to experiencing these connections likewise depends on one's worldview. It may be through meditation, prayer, study of holy works, or any number of other acts of passion and focus, whether fly fishing, rock climbing, or appreciating the arts.

Figure 2.7. *Transcendence is where you find it (by Ales Krivec, Slovenia [CC0], via https://unsplash.com/@aleskrivec).*

The path to transcendence does not rely so much on how it is achieved as on where it takes the practitioner. One tried-and-true path to these understandings is of course through religion, with thousands of years of collective history helping individuals experience the divine. Yet religions, like any human institution, are vulnerable to human fallibility and have often been responsible for more than their share of transgression: corruption, xenophobia, misogyny, coercion, and, occasionally, war, torture, and genocide. Just as we generally use fire for warmth and not to destroy, we do not discount a host of other conventions similarly responsible for their share of conflict: politics or economics, for example.[31] Similarly, we focus here on the aspects of faith that act to enhance community, honor, and understanding.

The question remains, though: What, precisely, *can* spiritual traditions offer the worlds of facilitation, mediation, and conflict transformation, especially when people in conflict often come from a variety of backgrounds and belief systems? Well, quite a lot, it turns out. Later we will explore the constructs of anger and conflict, as understood by faith traditions, and some of the tools and techniques to assuage both. I focus on the understandings and tools that have some universal application, precisely because of the need to resonate with those in conflict, regardless of their backgrounds and belief.

One example:

As noted above, approaches to the balance between the individual and the community can be thought of very differently in the North and West as compared with the South and East. These views play out in approaches to legal principles and conflict resolution as well. For example, the Western legal structure is very comfortable with the idea that one side in a dispute can be found entirely right and gain everything, while another side is found entirely wrong and loses everything.[32] In contrast, the balance of justice and mercy in many communities of the South and East can retain individual rights *and* honor on both sides of a dispute and lead to reconciliation of a wrongdoer within one's community. Consider the Arabic word *tarrahdhin*, for example, defined as "resolution of a conflict that involves no humiliation," a profound concept with no Western equivalent.

This is not a theoretical concept but rather put in practice throughout the Muslim world once a wrong has been committed through the ceremony of a *sulha*, a ritual ceremony of forgiveness. The term comes from *musalaha*, reconciliation, which implies that hostilities are ended, honor reestablished, and peace restored in the community.[33] This custom, which consists of private and often mediated negotiation of redress between the affected parties, is followed by a public declaration of forgiveness and, usually, a festive meal. Once the *sulha* is performed, the slate is wiped clean; it is as if the dispute never happened. The agreement is legally binding on both the individuals and the community. Grudges are dissuaded, and reference to past disputes may not be made to gain position in a current conflict.[34]

The balance of rights and honor, of justice and mercy, and its contrast to the Western construct of justice, is described by Jabbour:[35]

This is how [social] justice should be achieved. The courts condemn the guilty party in vain, because they never take care of the harm. Magistrates and police don't know what social justice is.

Figure 2.8. Prayer, Bangladesh *(by Shaeekh Shuvro [CC BY-SA 2.0], via Wikimedia Commons from Wikimedia Commons).*

Honor is an alien virtue. They believe in the virtue of punishment, but forgiveness is overshadowed and neglected, because peace-making is not on their minds.

The Western world seems to be lacking in just such a ritual ceremony of forgiveness, one that balances the needs of the individual with that of the community. A public ceremony would allow the community affected by a dispute—the stakeholders on all sides—to celebrate its resolution and thereby take ownership of seeing to its implementation.[36]

The idea of inherent balance between rationality and spirituality, self and community, rights and responsibilities, mind and heart heavily underlies approaches to transforming conflicts in indigenous and spiritual communities around the world (we'll learn more details in chapter 7). Carlo Osi, a lawyer trained in both the United States and his native Philippines, eloquently contrasts indigenous dispute resolution processes and Western ADR:

Even before the advent of formal ADR bodies and procedures in mainstream society, Indigenous peoples have long used ADR-like mechanisms—also referred to as Indigenous Dispute Resolution— to resolve existing rows between their own membership, with other tribes or with newer settlers. These involve Indigenous paradigms, beliefs and "Aboriginal Wisdom." Disputes are resolved based on the Indigenous community's culture and custom. These include traditional teachings, respect, relationships, interconnectedness, spirituality, prayers, storytelling, "saving face," recounting of facts and emotions. Group consensus is the goal to be achieved, as well as the maintenance of good relations with other community members, solidarity and reciprocal obligations—also known as K'e in the Navajo culture.

We have clearly seen the hazards of ignoring the relationship between rationality and spirituality but also the potential an integrated approach may offer for effective negotiations and conflict transformation.

As the historically contrasting worldviews of the global North and West and the South and East increasingly interact, both within and without the worlds of complex negotiations, we have the opportunity to heal historic divisions. The history of conflicts and cooperation suggests that people do come together, even across vociferous divides. And yet the suffering created by scarcity and conflict will only increase with population growth, poverty, and global change. As the dangers grow, however, so do the opportunities for dialogue and healing.

As someone who works primarily in water conflicts, I was especially heartened when, in 1996, the Episcopal Diocese in Massachusetts shifted its diocese boundaries from political divisions to watershed boundaries. The rationale was instructive:

> Simply demonstrating that we are all connected by water: rich and poor, urban and rural, upstream and downstream, is a fine place to start.

> I think the Holy Spirit will take care of the rest.[37]

Both faith and water ignore separations and boundaries. Thus, they offer vehicles for bringing people together, and because they touch all we do and experience, they also suggest a language by which we may discuss our common future.

CHAPTER THREE

Four Worlds and Four Scales

better:
see description in
UNESCO-IHP 2016

> *Techniques employ four qualities that reflect the nature of our world. Depending on the circumstance, you should be: hard as a diamond, flexible as a willow, smooth-flowing as water, or as empty as space.*
>
> Morihei Ueshiba, founder of the
> Japanese martial art of Aikido

There's a succinct thought experiment I use as a teaching tool in my water policy classes: Two people are stuck in a desert, and they only have enough water for one to survive. Who gets the water?

The ensuing discussion usually centers on assigning characteristics to the two individuals to try to elicit values about who might have a better right to live. Is one older than the other? Is one a parent? Could one contribute more to society? How would that be measured?

Occasionally, the concept of equity is raised: If they can't both live, then should both die?

Only rarely are characteristics of water invoked, generally when one notes that the discussion was focusing on only one aspect: the physical manifestation of water and its role in physical survival. But we know intuitively that water has other manifestations, which generally rise once the subject of death is broached. Clearly physical water is necessary for a good (or any) life, but what sort of water might aid in a good death? For example, one might think of emotional water, the joy that might be derived from even a small sip even as one is parched and approaching death

34

from dehydration. There is water experienced at an intuitive or perceptual level, water that connects to all else in the universe, reflections on which might help prepare one for a journey to the next stage in one's existence. And finally there is spiritual water, the few drops that might help one prepare for prayer or last rites.

Although our instinct is to default to the primacy of physical survival and the role that the physical characteristics of water could play in that goal, for some it is equally if not more important to think about how one might die and how the emotional, perceptual, and spiritual aspects of water could aid along that path.

Figure 3.1. Holy water font at the entrance of a Catholic church (© 2016 Sean P. Davis. Used with permission).

Understanding these four aspects, here of water but for that matter of anything—the physical, emotional, perceptual, and spiritual dimensions—turns out to have immensely deep roots from traditions around the world. Moreover, their manifestation in ourselves and in our interactions helps guide healing paths through the transformation of discord at a variety of scales. For both their universality and their utility in conflict transformation, we will spend some time getting to know them better. A lot better.

But first, an example.

The Four Worlds in the *Suk*

So you're traveling somewhere in the Middle East or North Africa, and you head to the local *suk*, or market, to check out the carpets. As you meander through the hot, winding alleyways, cardamom and *za'atar* wafting on the slight breeze, you finally spot a shop that looks promising. Colors and textures overflow the entranceway, and you eye pile after pile of carpets in all sizes and shapes draped throughout the shop.

As you are engulfed by the coolness of the shop's interior, your eyes naturally wander to find the likeliest target of your interest. Back home, the first words out of your mouth, perhaps before you even make eye contact with the shopkeeper, might be, "How much is that?" Here you don't even get to ask the question before the shopkeeper appears, urging you to a comfortable chair, assistant in tow bringing cool drinks and light snacks for your pleasure. Before anything, your *physical* needs are being attended to.

The shopkeeper will probably lead you into conversation about your home town, your travels and family—seemingly about anything *except* carpets. You're together attending to your *emotional* needs, bonding into a relationship.

As the conversation winds and wanders, your gaze likewise drifts until it sets upon *the* rug, the one whose colors match perfectly the décor in your living room, whose textures evoke precisely both your travels and your sense of home. The shopkeeper notices your interest, and the conversation steers around to rest on the rug. After learning the history of the carpet—its weave, patterns, and region of origin—and after protestations

Figure 3.2. *Carpets from a bazaar in the medina of Monastir, Tunisia (by Vivaystn [Own work] [CC BY-SA 3.0, cropped and desaturated from the original], via Wikimedia Commons from Wikimedia Commons).*

that money could not possibly be an issue with something so beautiful, you do eventually start to talk about price. The bargaining that ensues is partly *intellectual*, each of you calculating the point at which you can afford to buy or sell. But because of your new relationship, the exercise is also partly *intuitive*—a "knowing" and sharing of each other's needs and desires—almost a feeling of merging the needs of self and of other. For lack of a better term for this mental combination of intellectual and intuitive, we refer to this as a *perceptual* process.

Finally, a mutually acceptable price is agreed upon. You got a good deal, and the shopkeeper made a modest profit. You drink and talk a bit more as your carpet is wrapped for travel, then handshakes and smiles all around. "Go with God," the shopkeeper calls after you, passing on this blessing to see to your *spiritual* protection.

It's been an amazing afternoon. You're as delighted with your new acquisition as you are with the budding relationship that's been formed. You know you're comfortable and satisfied.

What you don't know is that, along with the trip to the *suk*, you've also traveled a well-worn path through four worlds and experienced a bit of transformation in the process.

Roots and Universality

This chapter describes in more detail the path that our carpet shopper experienced briefly in the *suk*, the idea that we might at any time experience the world around us through four distinct lenses, or states: a physical state, which we will later refer to through its Meso-American icon, a serpent; an emotional state, or jaguar; a perceptual, or knowing state, whose icon is a hummingbird; and a spiritual or connected level, an eagle. As we'll see in later chapters, these states exist within us and between us; working with them offers guidance to understanding both conflicts and their transformation.

First, let's look at some of their manifestations throughout history.

In Jewish tradition, Moses experienced the four worlds through four levels of holiness on his path to receive the Law on Mount Sinai.[1] After 3 days of intense spiritual preparation, all the Children of Israel were brought together to the foot of the mountain, atop which thunder, lightning, and blasts from the ram's horn signaled God's presence.[2] There, Moses had an altar built and sacrifices made among the nation as a whole. This experience of physical construction and sacrifice with the entire nation represents the first level, that of physical holiness.

At God's command, Moses then ascended higher, with only Aaron, his sons, and seventy elders, all of whom "beheld God, and they ate and drank."[3] Commentators[4] suggest that their joy was as great as the utmost pleasure and that they ate and drank in grateful celebration of this divine privilege. This level of the mountain itself, then, represents the second level: emotional holiness.

God then told Moses to go on alone to the peak of the cloud-covered mountain where, in a moment of pure consciousness, Moses received the Law in its entirety: "Ascend to Me to the mountain and remain there, and I shall give you the stone Tablets and the teaching and the commandment that I have written, to teach them."[5] The focus on the Law being transmit-

Figure 3.3. *Mount Sinai in Egypt (by Tamerlan at Polish Wikipedia [Public domain, desaturated from the original], via Wikimedia Commons from Wikimedia Commons).*

ted to Moses to "teach them" brings him to the third level: perceptual, or intuitive, holiness.

Finally, the thickness of the cloud itself (*'av ha'anan*), the divine presence at the summit of Mount Sinai, represents the fourth level: spiritual holiness.

Once the Children of Israel settled in the Land of Israel, this path through the four levels of holiness was recreated in the physical structure of the holy Temple in Jerusalem, corresponding to the gate of the Temple Courtyard, the interior of the Courtyard, the inner chamber of the Temple and, finally, the Holy of Holies, the seat of the divine presence.

(Interestingly, Angkor Wat, built roughly between 1116 and 1150 CE in modern-day Cambodia, has a similar structure, moving inward and upward from four surrounding towers through three worlds, with the fourth world represented at the top of the central tower originally with a statue of the Hindu god Vishnu, and since the temple's orientation to Buddhism, an empty space with a red sash. The reliefs of each level change from everyday scenes, then to a depiction of the Hindu creation story of the churning of the Sea of Milk, to temple dancers, and finally to "emptiness." Like Mount Sinai, the top of the central tower, built to emulate Mount Meru, the mythical home of the gods beyond the Himalayas, represented the point where "secular and sacred power joined forces."[6])

Thus, the Temple in Jerusalem was, in effect, a permanent recreation of the Sinai experience, which was intended to remain with the Jewish people throughout their history.[7]

With the destruction of the Temple in 586 BCE, and with prophecies of destruction of its successor and four lengthy exiles, it became clear that Jewish history would outlast this physical recreation of the path to revelation. In what would become one of the most inspired and democratizing acts in theologic history, the Sages of the Great Assembly inscribed this path to spiritual fulfillment within the structure of the Jewish prayer service, essentially crafting the service as a guided meditation through the four worlds, an inner journey through the courtyards of the Temple and ascension of the face of Sinai.

Figure 3.4. (a) *Model of Herod's Temple, Jerusalem (by Berthold Werner [Public domain, desaturated from the original], via Wikimedia Commons from Wikimedia Commons); and (b) Angkor Wat temple complex in Cambodia (by Benjamin Smith from United States [CC BY 2.0, desaturated from the original], via Wikimedia Commons from Wikimedia Commons).*

In essence, then, religious Jews who pray the thrice-daily prayer service follow this guided meditation through the four worlds every day, morning, noon, and night.[8]

(Psychologists will recognize Maslow's [1943] hierarchy of needs in the four worlds: physiological; safety, love, and belonging; esteem; and self-actualization. Abraham Maslow, son of immigrant Jews and surrounded by Jews as an adult in both his personal and professional lives, could easily have been exposed to these concepts. Although I have not seen any direct reference linking his hierarchy of needs to the Judaic four worlds, there is just too much similarity to ignore.)

BOX 3.1

FOUR EXILES AND FOUR WORLDS

Jewish history itself is said to follow a path through the four worlds: the Midrash (commentary on scripture) describes Jews experiencing four corresponding exiles in advance of the final redemption, each with an attack on one of the four aspects of our being:

- The Babylonian exile, a physical attack, including massacre, destruction, and removal from the land
- The Persian exile, attacking emotional holiness through licentiousness and promiscuity
- The Greek exile, with its premise that the intellect and faith are incompatible
- The Roman exile, which extends until today

This last is considered the most dangerous, because it suggests that our inherent hunger for spirituality can be satiated instead with materialism.

Rabbi Bentzion Milecki notes that each of these aspects to our being has its place "in the service of G-d: We need to serve G-d with a healthy body. Our emotions and our desires can and should be used for the greatest acts of holiness. And of course, intellect—especially the advances of science, technology, and communication—empower us as individuals and enable the masses to reach spiritual knowledge that was until now unattainable."[a]

a. "Lessons from the Dreidel," Kabbalah Online, Chabad.org. http://www.chabad.org/kabbalah/article_cdo/aid/1693257/jewish/Lessons-from-the-Dreidel.htm.

About one hundred years after the destruction of the Temple in Jerusalem, auspicious events took place 3,000 miles to the east, where the upper Ganges plain abuts the Himalayan highlands. The young prince Siddhartha, 29 years old and shielded thus far by his protective father from the outside world, set out on a certain day from his parents' home for the first time and was startled by the suffering he experienced in the famous Four Sights. On this chariot ride through the streets of Kapilavastu, he saw an aged man, who represented physical decay, or *annika*, impermanence; a sick person, who experienced *dukha*, suffering; a corpse, suggesting the powerful idea of *annata*, that the link between being and nonbeing is tenuous; and finally an ascetic, a holy man who devoted himself to a spiritual understanding of the roots of suffering.[9,10]

According to some traditions, the meditation that the Buddha practiced 6 years later on the evening of his enlightenment, known in Pali as *ānāpānasati*, or "mindfulness with breathing" and laid out in his *ānāpānasati Sutta*, followed a fourfold path that mirrored the Sights: contemplation of, in order, *kāya*, body; *vedanā*, feeling; *citta*, mind; and *Dhamma*, spirit.

> When the Blessed One sat at the foot of the Bodhi Tree and resolved not to rise until he had reached enlightenment, he took up *anapana sati* as his subject of meditation. On the basis of this, he attained the four *jhanas*,[11] recollected his previous lives, fathomed the nature of *samsara*,[12] aroused the succession of great insight knowledges, and at dawn, while 100,000 world systems trembled, he attained the limitless wisdom of a Fully Enlightened Buddha.[13]

Similarly, the heart of Buddhism, the Four Noble Truths, mirror these revelations, in order: 1. All is impermanent (physical); 2. The source of suffering is craving (emotional); 3. *Nirvana* is the cessation of suffering (knowing); 4. The path to *nirvana* is the eightfold path (spiritual).[14]

The commonality between the cores of these two traditions may not be surprising, given their relative proximity and the trade routes that have passed between them for millennia. Neither would the fact that we find identical constructs in Islam and in Hinduism, the former having had access to Judaism and the Hebrew Bible,[15] the latter a profound influence on the spiritual culture into which the Buddha was born. In Hinduism

Figure 3.5. *Photo of a painting in a Laotian temple depicting the four heavenly messengers (by Sacca [Public domain, desaturated from the original], via Wikimedia Commons from Wikimedia Commons).*

we learn about the sequence as body, mind, intellect, and AUM, or unity. Each deity can express each of these four aspects. Consider Vishnu's four totems—a mace (physical strength), a lotus flower (the glory of existence), a discus (representing the mind *chakra*), and the conch (representing AUM through the primeval sound of creation)—yet all are aspects of, "the nameless, formless, and attributeless Reality."[16]

In Islam, the bounded, physical expression of the path to holiness is most commonly manifested through *Sharia*, the law as derived from the Quran. To the physical path of *Sharia*, the Sufis, mystics of the Muslim world,[17] add three that each build on those before: *Tarikah*, the inner practice, expressed with deep emotion through love for each other and for God; *Hakika*, or truth, the direct understanding of the divine presence;

Figure 3.6. Painting depicting Vishnu (© www.astrogems.com, used with permission).

BOX 3.2

THE THIRD WORLD: WHEN WORDS OBSCURE IDEAS

Getting a real sense of the third world, what I have been calling "perceptual" or "knowing," can be confounded by the limits of our English vocabulary. In essence, it refers to what happens in the mental sphere, a rough combination of the intellectual activity that one might associate with the left side of the brain with the intuitive capacity of the right. Some traditions are explicit in a more nuanced vocabulary. Vipassana Buddhist practice prescribes mindfulness with two mental capacities: focused attention, a true concentration that is a "wholesome one-pointedness of mind," and insight, an intuitive awareness of higher truths.

Chassidic Judaism describes three ways of knowing: *chochma*, intuitive wisdom, *binah*, rational understanding, and *da'at*, the integrative knowledge "of God's presence in, with, and as all reality that arises from the merger of the two."[a] (Note these three form the acronym *Chabad*, the name of a well-known Chassidic movement.) This triad probably captures the third mental world best, and I hope this is what is conveyed by "knowing" or "perceptual."

a. *Rami M. Shapiro and Rabbi Zalman M. Schachter-Shalomi,* Tanya, the Masterpiece of Hasidic Wisdom: Selections Annotated & Explained *(Woodstock, VT: SkyLight Paths Pub., 2010).*

BOX 3.3

THE ORDER OF THE FOUR

These concepts too can often be confounded by the limits of our vocabulary, as exhibited in the relative order of the four worlds. For our purposes, we use the order of physical, emotional, perceptual, spiritual to suggest activity that is centered around the body, heart, mind, and spirit in order. But several faiths talk about heart–mind as one, and that it is actually the heart where thinking and especially intuition take place. So the order I describe here from Sufism comes from some sources, but others reverse the order of *Tarikah*, emotion, and *Hakika*, truth.[a] Similarly, as described later in this chapter, the delineations and order of the second and third worlds with both North and South American roots are fluid. We will talk more about the relationship between the heart and mind in chapter 6.

a. See, for example, Muhammedinur.com, "Shariat-Tarikat-Marifat-Hakikat," http://www.muham medinur.com/En/islam/shariat-tarikat-marifat-hakikat.html.

---

and *Marifah*, the deep attunement with God, as intuited through "the eye of the heart."[18]

Meanwhile in the Americas, whose people had at the time of the Buddha's enlightenment already been cut off by rising seas from the three "known" continents for 12,000 years, similar foundational teachings existed. The Four Worlds Development Project,[19] for example, describes the construct of the medicine wheel of the sacred tree as an ancient symbol used by almost all the Native people of the Americas:[20]

> The medicine wheel teaches us that we have four aspects to our nature: the physical, the mental, the emotional, and the spiritual. Each of these aspects must be equally developed in a healthy, well-balanced individual through the development and use of volition (i.e., will).[21]

Alberto Villoldo[22] describes how the knowledge of the Laika Earthkeepers, precursors of the Incas, "originated in sanctuaries high in the Himalayas and was brought to the Americas by the audacious travelers," who crossed the land bridge from Asia. He associates each of the Shamanic four levels of perception with its sacred totem: the level of Serpent,

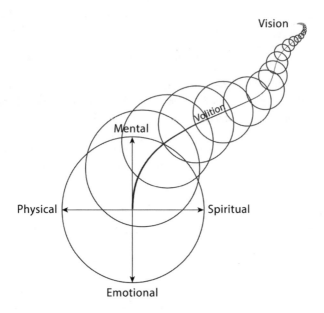

Figure 3.7. *"We can use our will to help us develop the four aspects of our nature" (from Julie Bopp et al.,* Sacred Tree: Reflections on Native American Spirituality *[Twin Lakes, WI: Lotus Press, 1984], p. 14. Used with permission).*

the body and physical perception; Jaguar, the mind and emotional perception; Hummingbird, the soul and sacred perception; and Eagle, spiritual perception. Villoldo associates each level with a set of *chakras*, which he describes as "domains of manifestation of vibration and light."[23]

Regardless of whether the four worlds originate from one source (or Source) or many, or whether, as both Rabbi Zalman Schachter-Shalomi[24] and Alberto Villoldo[25] suggest, we are hard-wired to experience the world through these lenses,[26] the sheer universality and practicality of the framework provides a solid foundation on which to develop a working model for our work.

Experiencing the Four Worlds

The most effective path to understanding the four worlds depends on how you learn best (see box 3.5 for an exercise, especially if you are an experiential learner). If visual models help, take a look at figure 3.8. If you were to look down on the figure in a map view, each state would be within the

BOX 3.4

FROM SERPENT TO SPIRIT EXERCISE

Many terms can evoke strong feelings that can impede their effectiveness. We've noticed in our workshops, for example, that the serpent can come with lots of mythic baggage, often associated with physical or even ethical sliminess, probably harking back to Genesis. Yet here we use the serpent simply to represent the rooted, bounded, physical components of the world. Interestingly, for Hindus of the Ramakrishna order, the serpent is a symbol of the spiritual level, as attained through raja yoga: concentration and meditation, "which arouse the 'serpent' of spirituality."[a]

Conversely, the word *spirituality* may also trigger strong feelings, particularly if one is secular or formerly religious (or, for that matter, particularly religious). Here, we use the term for its intuitive evocation of a deep yet ethereal connection with the forces of the universe. We definitely distinguish between religion and spirituality: We all know people who are spiritual without being religious and vice versa. I have had various relations with the concept as well, and I agree only that there is power in both transcendence and transformation.

As an exercise, notice which words trigger emotions in you, and try to pay close attention to what precisely is being triggered. What does it feel like? What stories might be behind these feelings? Try to assign your own name to your relationship and, once you've named it and honored it, see if you can set it aside and identify how the terms are being used by others. While still respecting your own relationship with these terms, can you work with them in the way intended by others?

a. *Swami Vivekananda*, The Complete Works of Swami Vivekananda, Volume 7, Conversations and Dialogues *(1907 [original publication date], online at Wikisource: https://en.wikisource.org/w/index .php?title=The_Complete_Works_of_Swami_Vivekananda/Volume_7/Conversations_And_Dialogues &oldid =4900933).*

other; each expands out from and incorporates the previous state. Yet from the side, they also rise—not because higher is better but because higher is higher. (In some traditions, as we've noted, each state is associated with different chakras, each ascending from the one before. As we'll note later, each can be "felt" in a different part of the body in ascension.)

A key point to understand about the worlds is that they exist all the time, simultaneously. One intuitive example might be seen through a piece of bread, which exists most recognizably on a physical plane, or if one is hungry and the bread is particularly good, one perceives the bread emotionally. One can also intellectualize the bread and consider its com-

Figure 3.8. *The four worlds (figure by David Reinert, Oregon State University, 2016).*

ponents and interaction with our body to provide sustenance. Finally, one might say a blessing over the bread, rendering it a source of spiritual nourishment. Although these four levels of perception can be thought of separately, and they might occasionally be achieved in sequence, they should not be considered as distinct or linear. The bread, in this example, exists simultaneously in all four states; it is up to us to determine through which lenses it will be perceived. Nonetheless, understanding the four worlds in sequence is often useful, if not critical. Someone desperately hungry, for example, may have difficulty taking the time and effort to intellectualize anything when offered a piece of bread.

Another point is that one state is not "better" than any other. The object is not to get to the "higher" states; each state has its place and vital role. Even the most focused ascetic, rock climber, or fly fisher, experiencing near-transcendent clarity, needs to make sure the physical body is nourished.

By focusing rather on process, tapping into the four perceptual states and, more importantly, the transformation that takes place when moving through and between them, we feel we can more readily engage the healthy energy of conflict and work toward transformation of individuals, groups, and complex systems.

This construct seems particularly useful for our purposes, engaging

Figure 3.9. Spiritual Bread *(painting by Orit Martin [www.oritmartin.com]. Used with permission).*

conflict regularly across cultural and political boundaries. Smith[27] notes the near-universality of the construct, what in summarizing religions' common vision he calls the "levels of reality." Figure 3.10 shows Smith's levels: body, heart, mind, and spirit.

Four States, Four Scales

From time immemorial, these four foundations have been understood at a variety of scales, from the minute to the universal. At an intimate scale, for example, both Jewish and Christian exegeses understand biblical text at four levels, paralleling the four worlds. In the Jewish *Pardes* (orchard) model,[28] each word, phrase, or sentence in holy text can be understood at any of four possible levels,[29] echoed in Catholic four levels of meaning, which date back at least to the second century CE: literal, allegorical,

BOX 3.5

TRAVELING THE FOUR WORLDS EXERCISE[a]

If you learn best by experiencing, all the descriptions in this chapter will have given you only a superficial taste of what these four states mean. This exercise is designed to offer a personal journey through the states, as a first pass at being able to work with them.

You'll need a friend to help you with this, ideally someone who is articulate and can act passionately about ideas. And definitely someone you trust.

Sit with your friend in a quiet location where you won't disturb anyone. Close off distractions and turn off your phone. Now, choose a topic of current events, something that you feel very strongly about (but *not* one that has even the slightest possibility of evoking personal trauma in your life). Which side of the issue do you identify with?

Now, ask your friend to argue as passionately as possible, taking the opposite position. But here's the trick: You are not allowed to say a word for 4 full minutes. Just listen. But try to really listen, even though it will be hard. Even though your friend may not (or, if he or she is your friend, probably does not) believe in the position they are taking, encourage them to argue it as forcefully and as clearly as possible.

As you listen, try to also notice carefully what's going on inside you.

Don't read further until you've completed the exercise.

What's more than likely is that the first thing you'll notice as you listen to difficult ideas is physical discomfort. Your muscles may tense up, especially your legs; your breathing and pulse will quicken, and you might feel your pores open as you sweat slightly. Your jaw and fists might clench involuntarily.

Almost simultaneously, you'll notice your feelings, probably strong and negative. You might feel anger, somewhere in the pit of your belly and your chest. You'll feel frustration, maybe in your shoulders and neck, at not being able to respond. You might, despite yourself, feel some admiration for your friend, for articulating so ardently concepts that you're pretty sure he or she does not believe.

Next might come something both surprising and interesting. If you're really listening—*really* listening—you might at some point actually feel a palpable shift in your perception. As you hear difficult ideas so clearly articulated, some part of you might relax the defenses of your physical and emotional shields enough to be intellectually curious about the other side and the beginnings of a readiness to intuit connections between what you thought existed only as two mutually exclusive sides. You'll feel this shift up around your head, but vaguely.

Most people's experience will stop somewhere in the first two or three levels. But if you're willing to lose yourself to the experience, and if you have practiced focusing acutely—maybe you pray or run or fish or meditate—you might have a brief, ethereal sense of connection, not just with the ideas and your friend but with the broader universe of all ideas and all friends. If you feel this at all, it might actually feel as if it is happening outside your physical body, perhaps just above and in front of you (although not quite).

When the 4 minutes are up, take some time to just sit quietly.

When you're ready, thank your friend, reflect, have a cup of tea. You might actually have some vestige of anger, so remember that it was "only" an exercise and disconnect your friend from the position he or she took on your behalf.

a. This exercise is modified from one developed by the Harvard Negotiation Project and taught by Erica Fox, director of the Harvard Negotiation Insight Initiative at the Program on Negotiation: http://www.pon .harvard.edu/. Used here with permission.

tropological, and anagogic.[30] In fact, the Catechism itself has four similar touchstones:

> The plan of this catechism is inspired by the great tradition of catechisms which build catechesis on four pillars: the baptismal profession of faith (the *Creed*), the sacraments of faith, the life of

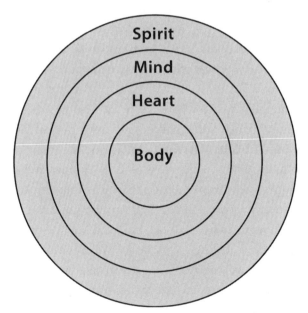

Figure 3.10. *Smith's "levels of reality" (figure by David Reinert, Oregon State University, 2016).*

faith (the *Commandments*), and the prayer of the believer (the *Lord's Prayer*).[31]

At the other scalar extreme, Kabbalistic understanding is that, because each individual is created in the image of the divine, the four worlds within the individual are connected to and mirror the four worlds of God's consciousness,[32] which in turn is basically a map of the structure of the universe.[33]

In more recent and more secular constructs, we will find echoes of these states in scales well beyond that of the individual. Rothman's[34] ARIA model for conflict resolution, which we'll use in detail in chapter 7, describes the potential for transformation in a negotiation or small group setting; Scharmer's[35] Theory U, a double fourfold matrix, was developed to elucidate the evolution and projection of institutions. Both draw on the four worlds.

Ken Wilber's[36] "Theory of Everything" is built around Huston Smith's summary of four "levels of reality," as seen in figure 3.11, what he refers to as body, heart, mind, and spirit. Wilber then superimposes a quadrant, where each quartile represents a different scale of humanity and worldview. The top half represents the individual, and the bottom half represents the collective; the left half is interpretive or unbounded, and the right half is empirical, positivistic—what we might think of as right and left brain, respectively.

The top left, individual–interpretive, he calls "I," representing internal consciousness. Wilber identifies philosophers who work at this scale ranging from Freud to Buddha. The top right, individual–empirical, which he calls "it," includes philosophers such as B. F. Skinner and John Locke. The bottom right, collective–empirical, which he calls "its," includes Karl Marx and system theorists. In the bottom left, collective–interpretive, called "we," Wilber includes Thomas Kuhn and Max Weber.

Similarly, in the following chapters, we will describe how a fourfold path might apply to each of the four scales to help inform transformative processes at each. Our scales include the following (see figure 3.12):

- Intrapersonal: what happens within each of us while engaged in processes of conflict, and how we can better guide our intentions

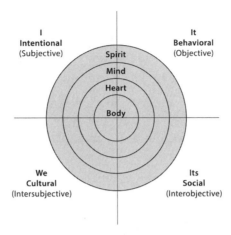

Figure 3.11. *Wilber's "Theory of Everything" (redrawn from Wilber, 2000).*

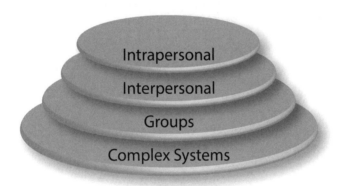

Figure 3.12. *Four scales of transformation (figure by David Reinert, Oregon State University, 2016).*

- Interpersonal: pairs and informal small groups, and how to use the states to engage more effectively

- Group settings: generally the traditional realm of classic ADR, the negotiation or discussion process, what happens "in the room"

- Complex systems: the "fuzzy" processes with huge uncertainties, where institutions evolve ponderously and transformative strategies include such imprecise tactics as "managing by intention" and being guided by the "precautionary principle"

Just as the perceptual states grow out and incorporate those before them, so do the scales at which we work. Individuals make up groups, which contribute to complex systems, and just as with the states, things get vaguer and "fuzzier" as we move outward. When we're at the scale of salmon recovery or global warming, neither the problems nor the solutions can be measured precisely, yet processes with echoes of the perceptual states can be tapped into to help with our understanding and approaches.

So that's the construct: four perceptual states, four scales. Let's get to work!

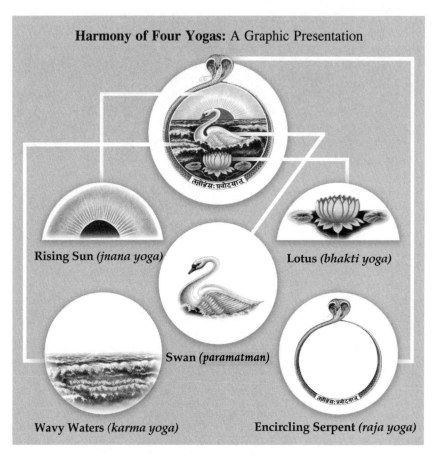

Figure 4.1. *The official emblem of the Ramakrishna order, a symbol of harmony and synthesis, was designed by Swamiji (see http://www.rkmissionchapra.org /emblem.php; used with permission).*

CHAPTER FOUR

Working with the Four Worlds

The crest of the Ramakrishna order was designed by Swami Vivekananda, who believed that life should be a harmonious blending of four yogas (paths to union): The rough water stands for karma yoga, for spiritual progress through unselfish work; the lotus for bhakti yoga, for development through love of God; and the rising Sun for jnana yoga, for the practice of discrimination and knowledge. All are held together by raja yoga, concentration and meditation, which arouse the "serpent" of spirituality. The swan in the center symbolizes the supreme soul.[1]

In 1990, as the Soviet Union was crumbling, Mikhail Gorbachev, its last president, made a speech to the Global Forum on Environment and Development for Survival in which he proposed that the environmental problems of the late twentieth century could best be addressed using a green analog to the diffuse medical emergency response model perfected by the Swiss—a "Red Cross for the environment." At the 1992 Earth Summit in Rio, the call was taken up. President Gorbachev was drafted as Green Cross International's founding president, and two topics were set as priorities: environmental problems that transcend national boundaries, with an emphasis on international waters, and the environmental vestiges of the arms race. (I actually got to brief the president on water issues in 1994 when he stopped briefly for a fundraiser in Los Angeles. My charge was to tell him all I thought was important about international waters. I was given 8 full minutes.)

Over the years, Green Cross International has been instrumental in bringing together representatives of countries that share waterways in politically tense basins around the world; often it is President Gorbachev's name and connections that help overcome barriers, and in May 2008 they cosponsored with the Peres Center for Peace just such a meeting between Israelis and Palestinians on the shores of Lake Geneva to help craft priorities for their shared water resources. (President Gorbachev and Israeli president Shimon Peres were apparently good friends, and Peres likewise was interested in how shared water resources can be a vehicle for dialogue.)

The name of the workshop that brought together about thirty water resource professionals delineated the nature of both the problem and the approach. "Defining Water Needs for Fully Exploited Resources" suggests two aspects. First, the region is simply out of water. Every drop that falls between the Jordan River and the Mediterranean is fully exploited; demand actually hit supply in 1968. And, second, the focus would be on prioritizing needs rather than rights, with an emphasis on demarcating priorities for actual uses rather than what one given side feels it "deserves."

The tenor of the conversation was cordial: The water folks in the region have worked across borders together for decades, even as hostilities raged over other issues. But an exercise in prioritizing water needs is surprisingly complex, even among water professionals. Although everyone understands that water goes for drinking, cooking, cleaning, agriculture, hydropower, ecosystem protection, esthetics, and spiritual purposes, it is unexpectedly tough to come to consensus over which use is more important than which. I've done this exercise in negotiations, workshops, and the classroom, and once we get into the details, there is generally very little agreement past drinking water, which most agree is the highest priority but generally accounts for a very low percentage of total use (about 5 percent globally).

So in Switzerland, and with no small credit to Prof. Eran Feitelson of Hebrew University, who had essentially crafted the exercise, all had decided in advance that they would focus on water needs, not rights. Everyone was running out, it was argued, and prioritizing what was needed would help facilitate a later discussion on legal rights. The problem was, what was needed? Farmers thought agricultural water was the most important, and industrialists argued that they actually contribute a higher percentage of gross domestic product with their water use. Environmentalists urged that both agricultural and industrial water took from the ecosystem, to everyone's detriment. And of course, Palestinians argued for more water for their uses, Israelis for theirs. There seemed to be no set of values that all could agree on to help guide the discussion.

Except there was . . . but it took a while to get there, along a route through four worlds.

Characteristics of the Four Worlds

What is it about the four worlds that is so universally powerful, and how can we tap that power for better conversations? Let's take a look at some characteristics of the four worlds with an eye toward using the framework in conflict transformation.

"Higher" Is Simply Higher

First, as noted in the previous chapter, "higher" levels do not mean better, but only higher in an energetic sense. Recall that in the traditions that invoke some model of chakras, or energy centers, the foci of each of these four foundations in an individual actually do ascend in order. Both Alberto Villoldo, a scholar and practitioner of the ways of the Shamanic "earthkeepers" of the Americas,[2] and Carolyn Myss, a pioneer in the field of "energy medicine,"[3] have clear, ecumenical descriptions of the chakras and their relationship to the four worlds (see figure 4.3).[4] In figure 4.3, Myss draws parallel structures between Hindu understanding of chakras, the Kabbalistic Tree of Life, and the Catholic sacraments, defining them in seven ascending layers. Daniel C. Matt, a Kabbalah scholar at the Graduate Theological Union in Berkeley,[5] in turn, maps the four worlds on the Tree of Life, showing where each level of consciousness transcends the former (see figure 4.5 later in this chapter).

For our purposes, understanding the nature of ascension will be useful. We'll note in the next chapter, for example, the exercise of moving the

Figure 4.2. *Baptisms at the Jordan River (by Ian Scott [CC BY-SA 2.0, desaturated from the original], via Wikimedia Commons from Wikimedia Commons).*

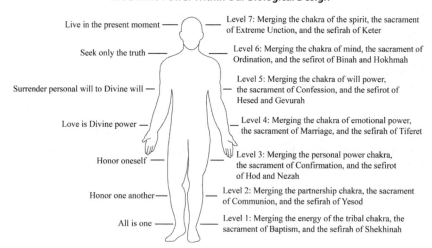

The Divine Power Within Our Biological Design

Live in the present moment — Level 7: Merging the chakra of the spirit, the sacrament of Extreme Unction, and the sefirah of Keter

Seek only the truth — Level 6: Merging the chakra of mind, the sacrament of Ordination, and the sefirot of Binah and Hokhmah

Surrender personal will to Divine will — Level 5: Merging the chakra of will power, the sacrament of Confession, and the sefirot of Hesed and Gevurah

Love is Divine power — Level 4: Merging the chakra of emotional power, the sacrament of Marriage, and the sefirah of Tiferet

Honor oneself — Level 3: Merging the personal power chakra, the sacrament of Confirmation, and the sefirot of Hod and Nezah

Honor one another — Level 2: Merging the partnership chakra, the sacrament of Communion, and the sefirah of Yesod

All is one — Level 1: Merging the energy of the tribal chakra, the sacrament of Baptism, and the sefirah of Shekhinah

Figure 4.3. *The* chakras, sacraments, and Kabbalistic *sefirot (from* Anatomy of the Spirit: The Seven Stages of Power and Healing, *by Caroline Myss, copyright © 1996 by Caroline Myss. Foreword copyright © 1996 by Crown Publishers, Inc. Used by permission of Harmony Books, an imprint of the Crown Publishing Group, a division of Penguin Random House LLC. All rights reserved).*

uncomfortable energy that comes with conflict within oneself upward and outward to where it can be addressed with greater ease.

The Order Is Useful but Not Inflexible

Similarly, understanding that the four worlds move from physical to emotional to perceptual to spiritual can provide guidance in the structure of conversation. In chapter 7, on groups, for example, we will note how in resource disputes, often addressing these four sets of needs in order can be key in achieving breakthroughs in negotiations.

Shamanic practitioner Alberto Villoldo observes that what is perceived as a problem at one level is actually an opportunity at the level above it,[6] further suggesting that solutions to problems are generally found at the level above. He gives the loss of a job as an example, naturally perceived initially as problematic, even catastrophic, but then often as an opportunity to reinvent oneself. Similarly, most conflict is initially viewed with concern, yet it often provides the excuse, attention, and resources for healthy conversations and problem solving, regularly leading to a better situation than before.

Four Worlds, Within and Without

In most structures of the four worlds, the first, or lower, three tend to be described as internal to the individual or group, whereas the fourth transcends boundaries. In the most literal meaning, one's physical and emotional lenses occur within the body, whereas the perceptual lens straddles internal and external, for example between intellectual and intuitive understanding. When one intellectualizes a difficult problem, it feels as if the thinking is happening internally (people often say something like "My head hurts" or "My brain feels full" when working too hard intellectually), yet flashes of intuition feel like brief contact with an external source.[7] Most spiritual practitioners suggest that the spiritual lens transcends the individual through contact with a larger connection. Similarly, the lower chakras are all described as being within the body, and the highest being just above and in front of the head.

This understanding of the relationship between internal and external will be extremely helpful at all scales, including interpersonal and group scales. The impact of conflict is generally felt by a much larger population than is charged with resolving it, so working with the relationship between "in the room" and "out of the room" will be critical. The workings of small groups of diplomats or stakeholders are critical when they are together, and they can also have far-reaching consequence well outside their meetings. Jay Rothman's[8] ARIA model for conflict resolution, which we will work with extensively in chapter 7, includes four phases of working through disputes: adversarial, reflexive, integrative, and action. These first three focus on those "in the room," whereas the last, action, requires thinking together about a plan to include also those not involved in dialogue.[9]

Distinctions and Their Disappearance

Boundaries and distinctions tend to dissolve as one moves through the levels. Moving upward and deeper has been described using the analogy of light through a prism. At the lower levels, we see light as if passed through a prism, noting the separate colors. As we move higher, those distinctions gradually disappear, and we experience colors more as a palette of gradations with no clear distinctions, until finally all colors dissolve into pure light. (Or darkness. Theologically, even that distinction eventually dissipates.[10])

So too energetically. Many traditions describe the apparent separateness of individuals and objects as illusory. As mentioned in chapter 2, one of Einstein's great contributions was that matter and energy are simply different manifestations of each other, and thus the entire universe is made up either of energy or of potential energy. Theologically, one might take the next step and offer that energy and consciousness are similarly manifestations of one another, which then suggests a universe entirely made up of consciousness or potential consciousness:[11]

> This is what he [the mythical discoverer of Toltec theology] discovered: Everything in existence is a manifestation of the one living being we call God. Everything is God. And he came to the conclusion that human perception is merely light perceiving light. He also saw that matter is a mirror—everything is a mirror that reflects light and creates images of that light—and the world of

Figure 4.4. *Water drops in the air act as tiny prisms, forming a rainbow, like this one at Antrodoco in Italy (by Alessandro from Rieti, Italy [CC BY 2.0, desaturated from the original], via Wikimedia Commons from Wikimedia Commons).*

illusion, the Dream, is just like smoke which doesn't allow us to see what we really are. "The real us is pure love, pure light," he said.[12]

How one moves from experiencing existence from its apparent, individualized perspective to grasp some inkling of the inherent interconnectedness of all that exists is the goal of many mystical paths. al-Jerrahi offers the explanation of the Sufi sage Ibn 'Arabi:

At the level of the law (*shariah*) there is "yours and mine." That is, the law guarantees individual rights and ethical relations between people. At the level of the Sufi path (*tariqah*), "mine is yours and yours is mine," the dervishes are expected to treat one another as brothers and sisters—to open their home, their hearts, and their purses to one another. At the level of Truth (*haqiqah*), there is "no mine and no yours." The advanced Sufis at this level realize that all things are from God. They are really only caretakers and "possess" nothing. At the level of Gnosis (*marifah*), "there is no me and no you." At this final level, the individual has realized that all is God, that nothing and no one is separate from God.[13]

Putting the Structure to Work

Working with conflict is working with energy. Thus, understanding energy's flows and levels, as well as the ephemeral boundaries that are as diverse between individuals as between nations, becomes critical as we learn to work through conflict.

Within us, we sense in our body where we feel, say, the anguish of problems at work and, alternatively, the joyful anticipation of seeing a loved one after an absence. As we participate in difficult conversations, either as a participant or as a facilitator, keeping one eye on the location and intensity of these internal feelings will be useful in crafting more healthful dialogues.

Between us, as individuals and in small groups, these energies interact. Anger meets anger and, with care, can be transformed into understanding. Learning to hear with our heart helps us to understand that anger or agitation is generally a shield protecting vulnerability, which in turn allows us to engage in a more healthful manner.

In groups, we usually focus on the boundaries that divide us. Even the concept of "stakeholder" suggests that the role of each individual is to represent some set of interests; we are in the room as "environmentalist" or "rancher" or "urbanite." Because these boundaries are generally artificial and ephemeral, addressing shared values helps lead us to common understanding and, often, to ways to work together through a perceived problem. The rancher cares deeply for the environment, and both the urbanite and the environmentalist are interested in a healthy economy. Focusing less on the boundaries and more on our shared values often points to our way forward.

In the following chapters, we will walk through each of these scales—within us, between us, and in groups—to see how working with the four worlds and their attributes can help inform better understanding and, ideally, better approaches for preventing and resolving even seemingly intractable conflict.

BOX 4.1

FOUR WORLDS IN THE HEBREW BIBLE

The Kabbalists offer examples in biblical history of those who have understood the diffusion of individuality at borders of each of the four worlds. The model suggests that, although we exist in the physical, separated world of *assiah*, action, with deep prayer, meditation, and perpetual effort at aligning our will with God's will, we may glimpse the next level of *yetzirah*, formation (figure 4.5). This comes with the first dissolution of distinctions, manifested for example through greater empathy and lovingkindness toward others. If we are interconnected, it becomes more difficult to hate or harm others, as we increasingly realize that we would be hating or harming ourselves.[a]

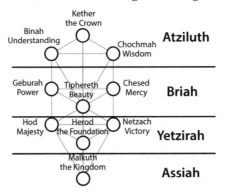

Figure 4.5. *The four worlds and the Kabbalistic Tree of Life (redrawn by David Reinert, Oregon State University, 2016, from notes from a course on Kabbalah by Dr. Shaiya Rothberg of the Conservative Yeshiva in Jerusalem, offered in 2004–05).*

The prophets are given as examples of those who glimpse the next world of *briah*, creation, where even the distinction between past and future dissipates, such that they can discern what will happen as if it already has. The Kabbalists give only one example of an individual who glimpsed the next level, *atziluth*, or emanation: Moses, who on Sinai grasped in one instant of pure clarity the structure and workings of the universe as a whole, intuiting the Torah in its entirety as a path for humanity to achieve holiness.

Other world traditions describe individuals with similar levels of transcendence; the Buddha, Jesus, and Mohammed, for example, are all described as achieving a level of enlightened insight into the divine nature of the universe.

a. *At this level and above, much Messianic and end-time prophesy can be understood: We would naturally "study war no more" (Isaiah 2:4 and Micah 4:3), and the wolf might well dwell with the lamb (Isaiah 11:6) (ArtScroll Chumash).*

Figure 4.6. *Stakeholder workshop in the Mekong River basin (photo courtesy of the author).*

Applying the Framework, from the *Suk* to Switzerland

Because this understanding seems to be universal, we find ready applications at all stages of conflict transformation. In conflict resolution process design, for example, how often do we even think about the physical component? Most negotiations I'm involved with take place in modern hotel meeting rooms, often windowless, with a seating structure seemingly designed to exacerbate hostilities. The four worlds remind us to think through each, starting with the physical: Would the meetings have a different feel in a different building, perhaps a church or community center? A group in California who found themselves shouting regularly solved that problem by moving their meetings to a public library. Is food offered? Can it be done with intention? Tribal representatives in discussions over water resources of the Columbia River invited negotiators to a First Foods Celebration, allowing them to demonstrate in a very tangible way the integration of the issues at hand with all aspects of their culture and society. And so on, from the physical through emotional, intellectual, and spiritual needs as well (we'll take each up in later chapters).

Designing processes to incorporate the four worlds becomes easier with a deep understanding of how they work within us individually and collectively and how they can have profound results.

Recall from the beginning of this chapter, our meeting in Switzerland between Israelis and Palestinians, as agriculturalists, environmentalists, and economists all maneuvered for their priorities while trying to determine what water uses were "needed."

After a discussion of the four worlds and how they are manifested in all major religions of the area, the discussion on priorities took an unexpected leap: There was general consensus that the highest priority should be given simultaneously to drinking water *and* to water for spiritual purposes: both the most basic and the "highest" use. This agreement was surprisingly unanimous and provided an immediate catalyst for the rest of the meeting. By agreeing that everyone, Israeli and Palestinian alike, all needed the same amount of water for survival, participants acknowledged the recognition and legitimacy that each side seeks. This point was reinforced by the simultaneous acknowledgment that each group's spirituality was respected by the group as a whole, a point brought home as in turn a Christian, a Muslim, and a Jew each described water's centrality to their practice.

This breakthrough had a transformative effect on the room and helped facilitate discussions all the way up the hierarchy of needs. The group prioritized first subsistence needs, whether agricultural or industrial (nuance that was not clear before the four worlds discussion); then water for critical ecosystems; then for commercial uses, whether industrial or agricultural; and finally for the environment at large.

An astonishing level of agreement was achieved in a relatively short amount of time, which then became the basis for subsequent research and negotiations.

~

Understanding these constructs and their universality leads to tremendous possibilities in the design and implementation of processes, training, collaborative learning, and intentional management. It allows a structure that moves through different lenses and perceptions while tapping into what seems to be a fairly universal set of needs. Finally, it allows a focus on transformative processes that bolster the limited success of emphasizing quantifiable benefits.

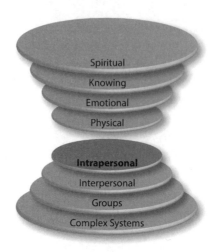

Figure 5.1.

Table 5.1
Four Worlds and
Foundational Needs

Physical
Emotional
Perceptual
Spiritual

Figure 5.2. Confluence of Kura and Araks rivers (by Hasanalizade [Own work] [CC BY-SA 4.0, desaturated from the original], via Wikimedia Commons from Wikimedia Commons).

CHAPTER FIVE

Two Wolves and the Storm Within: Transforming Internal Conflict

A Native American grandfather was talking to his grandson. He said, "I feel as if I have two wolves fighting in my heart. One wolf is vengeful, jealous, angry, and violent. The other wolf is loving and compassionate."

The grandson asked him, "Which wolf will win the fight in your heart?"

The grandfather answered, "The one I feed."

—A Cherokee Legend

Know thyself.   —Socrates

Learning to Be Screamed at in Russian

Relations between the states of Azerbaijan and Armenia in the Caucasus have been tense for decades. There is a long, strained history, including two wars in the last century and still-disputed territory between the countries. They do not have diplomatic relations, and they are technically in a state of war. Regardless, they are tied together by the Kura–Araks River basin, a system that both ignores the political boundaries between the countries and is heavily contaminated by chemical, industrial, biological, agricultural, and radioactive pollutants, vestiges of environmental mismanagement in the former Soviet Union.

So, despite the tensions and lack of relations after independence, water managers in both countries realized that they needed to work together to identify the details of the environmental hot spots if they were to have any chance of mitigating their impacts and thus help everyone within the basin access a cleaner system. Fortunately, Georgia—a country that has diplomatic relations with both Azerbaijan and Armenia—also shares the river system and thus also a real interest in addressing their shared water quality concerns.

And that is why, some years ago, Azeri, Armenian, and Georgian scientists and water managers gathered in an unpublicized set of meetings in unmarked rooms at the Marriott Hotel in downtown Tbilisi, Georgia.

As one of the facilitators, I could feel the tension in the air the minute I walked in the room, a fluorescent-lit, nondescript, windowless ballroom that could have been found in just about any international chain just about anywhere in the world. The thirty participants were almost all men, all trained in a technical field, all wearing dark suits, all sitting by their own countrymen, all looking down at whatever work they were pretending to do. At my request, they were seated around large round tables—not classroom or formal negotiation style—each with about six seats. Normally this arrangement helps to encourage conversation. It was not working.

We started off on a tense note, even before discussions formally began. The map that we passed out to work with had the territory disputed between Azerbaijan and Armenia marked "disputed territory."

"It's not disputed," argued the leader of the Azeri delegation. "It's Azerbaijan."

"It's not disputed," argued the leader of the Armenian delegation. "It's Armenia."

Neither side would work with the map as labeled, and all stewed in silence as we quickly ran off new maps with no human-delineated boundaries at all, just natural features.

With new maps in hand, I started off as I almost always do, with some simple ice-breaking exercises that involved moving around the tables, switching partners, and simulating arm wrestling. I learned these exercises from Terry Barnett, a master facilitator who worked extensively with the World Bank. I have since used them successfully all over the world, including with ministers and CEOs, as I know had Terry before his untimely passing in 2015.

Even though the language of the workshop was Russian, the language common to the three countries, the simultaneous interpretation to English coming to my earpiece from the booth in the back of the room seemed both fluid and fluent, and I felt more comfortable as the participants engaged.

And then they stopped. A leader of one of the delegations suddenly stood up, threw down his notebook, and started to shout across the room at me. Really loud. Really fast. In Russian.

While the interpreter did her best to keep up, the delegate's passion propelled him ever faster forward. But still, I got the gist from a couple of the sentences that came through.

"We're not kindergartners who came here to play kiddie games! We're scientists, and we're here to work!"

But to get a real sense, you have to imagine that theme repeated in myriad manifestations, with much more florid language, over almost 5 minutes. Really loud. Really fast. In Russian.

Appreciating what happened next is the focus of this chapter: understanding the conflict within or, to use the terms of scale, intrapersonal conflict.

Walking the Path Within

Before anyone tries to help anyone else with a conflict, whether formally as a mediator or facilitator, or informally between co-workers or friends, an honest self-assessment is in order: Do I have conflict inside of me about this issue or any of the participants, or other internal distractions, that preclude me from doing the work?

Here we explore ways to systematically examine this question and tools for moving forward if the answer is yes.

To illustrate: As a co-facilitator and I were about to walk into a room of representatives from Southeast Asian countries discussing a contentious potential dam in one of the countries, I quoted one of the participants, who had said something disparaging about dams in general. My colleague thought I was expressing my own views and wheeled on me there in the hallway.

"Aaron, can you live with all possible outcomes from the discussions in this room? Tell me now, because if not, I can't do this process with you."

What a great question! And one I had given precious little thought to before that. How often do we check in with ourselves and ask ourselves that type of question? And he was right. If my feelings about dams were too strong to facilitate, I simply would not do an honest job. People know when they are being led or steered in a particular direction, and it rarely ends well.

As chair of an academic department, I often cared deeply about the outcomes of discussions I was supposed to lead. After I had caught myself trying to gently "guide" an outcome toward one that I favored, and feeling the immediate and consequent backlash, I learned to either "care less"—that is, trust the people and the process—or to get out of the way. On occasion, I would simply turn running the meeting over to someone else and request that I be allowed to participate in that meeting as an advocate, not as chair. That transparency was usually enough to allow general acceptance of both roles. So basically, if you feel so strongly about an issue that it will hamper honest facilitation, you have two choices: Learn to care less or let someone else facilitate. (Or, as a trainee in a recent skill-building course described it, lead, leave, or suck it up.)

Likewise, one needs a similar self-assessment if one feels strong emotions (positive or negative) about any of the participants or the groups they represent. Similarly, one's own health and well-being matter. Too distracted to do the job well or step into the role? Then don't.

A Four Worlds Check-In

Observing and assessing how the four worlds within us interact and feed each other and how intrapersonal conflict can manifest within and between them are critical skills to learn. Equally if not more important is how to do the work at hand, whether in a formal or informal role, regardless of the raging of our internal world. Both sets of skills are discussed here. First, let's think about checking in on the worlds separately.

BOX 5.1

TAKEAWAY SKILLS

After an honest check-in of the worlds within, if you determine a potential intrapersonal conflict, you have three choices:

- Lead. That is, care less to the point where the conflict does not affect your leadership.
- Leave. Let someone else facilitate and either act as a participant or advocate or actually leave; don't participate at all.
- Suck it up. Own the dispute and determine to work through it regardless.

Physical

Bringing our attention to how and where in our bodies we experience our perceptions of what is going on around us is often a helpful approach to working through blocks that may arise. Naturally, facilitating any important issue requires that one be aware of physical impediments to being present energetically. A quick self-assessment can be useful, such as thinking through the impacts of jet lag or checking in on other issues in your body and your life. Are you healthy? Hungry? Cold? Hot? Will food be available for meals and breaks? Drinks? Restrooms?

What about the physical needs you will have to do the work you are called to do? Is the equipment working? Have you checked your slides to make sure they will show correctly on the system? Run through whatever physical objects you will need in the course of the day and make sure whatever you may need is available and working.

Emotional

The key question to ask yourself here is whether there is anything going on in your life that would impede your focus on the issues at hand. Are you grappling with family or professional issues of your own that may affect your skills? Do you have history with anyone else who will be in the room, or an organization that will be represented, that would challenge you emotionally? Ask honestly whether you have the emotional wherewithal to take on the tasks at hand. If not, see whether you can postpone or find a replacement.

Perceptual and Spiritual

As my co-facilitator asked me, can you live with all possible outcomes from the discussions in this room? Does the issue trigger any ethical concerns you have? Do you have a difficult history either with the issue or with any of the participants that could cloud your work? If any potential outcome would conflict profoundly with your worldview or spiritual life, it truly behooves you, and the process, to check whether someone else might be better in this role.

My friend and skilled facilitator Glen Hearns introduced me to the yogic concept of *satya*, which he defines as "being truthful—both to oneself (internal reflection) and then externally in your actions towards others and the outside world."

Many thinkers have described prescriptions for each of the internal worlds separately. In Villoldo's words,

> If you are sick, you can intervene at all four levels of perception: In serpent, you treat yourself with medicine; in jaguar, with psychology; in hummingbird, with meditation or spiritual practice; in eagle, with the awareness and wisdom of Spirit.[1]

The Worlds Swirling Within

Intrapersonal conflict manifested through any of the four worlds separately can be difficult to work through, but identifying the concern and determining its seriousness is fairly straightforward, as described above. More often, though, the intrapersonal worlds swirl together and interact, feeding each other for better or for worse. Working through these storms as they arise starts with awareness, letting your attention rest where it needs to be to keep you balanced between your internal workings and the world around you.

In the conflict management world, some work does exist on the tools a mediator or facilitator might draw on to monitor one's internal workings while leading a process. These are useful tools for anyone thinking about helping to intervene in conflictive settings, whether one is acting formally or informally, whether as a leader or participant. For example, as noted in chapter 2, the Association for Conflict Resolution (ACR) now has a spirituality section, and the fall 2005 issue of ACR's journal, *ACResolution*, is titled "Spirituality and the Heart of Conflict Resolution." The six key articles in the issue describe eloquently how their authors, all well-known practitioners,[2] understand the concept of spirituality and tap into some practice of mindfulness to stay connected. Leonard Riskin, now at the University of Florida, has taught mindfulness meditation to his law students for years,[3] Scott Rodgers keeps a website called *The Mindful Mediator*,[4] and Daniel Bowling and David Hoffman have edited a rich volume called *Bringing Peace into the Room*,[5] in which they examine the psychological, intellectual, and spiritual qualities of professional mediators for the most potent elements. In Erica Ariel Fox's wonderful book *Winning from Within*,[6] she draws explicitly on the four internal worlds in secular form: Warrior, Lover, Thinker, Dreamer.

At the heart of most of this work is mindfulness, the practice of bringing one's attention to whatever is unfolding in the present moment. Most faith traditions include mindfulness practice among their spiritual approaches. Hinduism gives us Yoga and its Eight Limbs as mindfulness practice, "unifying body, mind, and spirit."[7] Most forms of Christianity likewise have meditative traditions: the spiritual exercises of Saint Ignatius in Catholicism,[8] for example, or the use of religious icons as a focus of meditation by Orthodox Christians. Quaker prayer services are silent and meditative until someone in the congregation is called by their Inner Light to contribute, and Mormon mantras allow access to "the most secret, most sacred doors through which we pass into the presence of the Lord."[9] The *zikr* in the Muslim tradition—verbal repetition of a holy name or concept—offers a similar focus, just as some Jews use the divine manifestations of the Tree of Life.

Most Western descriptions of mindfulness practice, though, draw from Vipassana meditation techniques, which offer clear directions for assessing where internal issues may lie and how the assessment itself often helps alleviate obstacles. For example, Buddhist writings describe how to allow one's attention to settle on, in order, one's physical, emotional, intuitive, and spiritual centers, each connected with an energy center moving up through the body.[10] (Do the exercise in box 5.2 to get a sense of the physical manifestations of different sets of feelings and thoughts.)

EXERCISE

Find a comfortable spot to sit where, ideally, your legs are either crossed or firmly on the ground, your spine is straight, and your hands are comfortably in your lap. What follows is a guided meditation; you can read this yourself in advance and then do the exercise, or you can ask a friend to guide you through while your eyes are closed.

Let your attention rest on your breath for a while, either by focusing on the feeling of the air as it drifts in and out past the insides of your nostrils or by paying close attention to the feeling of contact with your shirt as your chest rises and falls with each breath. As your attention wanders, which it no doubt will, simply notice that it has wandered and gently bring your attention back to your breath. Don't attach emotion to the fact your mind wanders; just gently bring your attention back to your breath.

At some point, let your mind focus on this scenario: You are driving to a very important meeting where your presence is critical and you are running late. You are alone in your car, you are stuck in traffic, and your cell phone battery is dead. You are late, getting later, and there is simply nothing you can do about it.

As your mind is crafting this scenario, notice where in your body you feel the sensation of the story.

[*If you are alone, stop reading here and do this first part of the exercise. Only then, continue reading below.*]

Most people picturing this scenario describe some version of "a pit in the stomach," almost a queasiness deep in the center of one's being. As your mind's eye takes over and the details of the scenario become more elaborate, and as the potential consequences of missing the meeting become ever more dramatic, the discomfort can become more acute.

Now let your attention come back to your breath for a few moments.

When the discomfort has dissipated with the calming effects of simply noticing your breath, allow another scenario to unfold in your mind's eye:

You walk into a room where you are to take an exam, one that is crucial to your professional or academic advancement. Given the importance, you have studied for weeks for this exam and feel well prepared. As you walk in, take your seat, and turn the exam over to begin, you notice that nothing on the exam looks familiar. As you read further, you increasingly come to the realization that you have studied entirely the wrong material, you are not pre-pared in the least, and you are likely to fail.

Again, notice where in your body you feel the sensation of the story as it is unfolding.

[*Again, if you are alone, stop reading here and do this second part of the exercise. Then continue reading below.*]

For this scenario, people often feel the discomfort a bit higher in the body, generally a tension or tightening around the shoulders or neck. Some describe their "brain hurting."

What you are feeling are the chakras associated with two of the four worlds. The first story focuses on threats to your emotional being: embarrass-ment or challenges to your professionalism. Caroline Myss[a] describes this as the *Manipura chakra* of the Kundalini system, which holds lessons related to the ego, personality, and self-esteem. The second scenario centers on your per-ceptual well-being, where intellect and intuition meet in what Myss describes as the *Ajna chakra*, which holds lessons related to mind, intuition, insight, and wisdom.[b]

Notice the two sets of physical feelings—how they are similar, how they are different—and see whether the very act of letting your attention rest on the sensations helps to alleviate some of the discomfort.

a. *Caroline Myss,* Anatomy of the Spirit: The Seven Stages of Power and Healing *(New York: Three Rivers Press, 1996), follows Joseph Campbell's map of Kundalini chakras from* The Mythic Image *(Princeton, NJ: Princeton University Press, 1974).*

b. *If you crafted the second scenario as being work-related and focused on the feelings associated with potential failure at work rather than on the intellectual challenge, you may have experienced both scenarios similarly in the pit of your stomach.*

As noted in the exercise in box 5.2, if one is concerned with being late to an important meeting, for example, they would probably feel that in the emotional center, as a pit in the stomach. On the other hand, if the concern is about being ill prepared for an exam, that discomfort would probably be higher toward the intellectual center, perhaps as a stress at the base of the skull.

What is useful for our purposes is to notice that the story we weave in our heads fuels the discomfort we feel in our bodies and vice versa. The three internal worlds of the physical, emotional, and perceptual work together in a seemingly endless, self-perpetuating cycle. As the story be-comes more elaborate, the discomfort can grow, and the energy ends up

Figure 5.3. Stuck in traffic (by Raysonho @ Open Grid Scheduler / Grid Engine [Own work] [CC0], via Wikimedia Commons from Wikimedia Commons).

looking for an outlet where we might end up lashing out at those around us, even for something apparently unrelated.

And yet the very act of bringing our attention to the physical discomfort—exploring it in all its dimensions, closely observing exactly what it means to "feel" something—ends up cutting off its fuel. Attention can really only rest in one place at a time with any focus; therefore, if it is resting on the discomfort, it cannot contribute to the story that is fueling the discomfort. So the very act of closely examining the physical sensation can help alleviate the associated discomfort, often to a point where one can clearly and rationally make a decision, one that is *not* being led by the story or the pain.

So, for example, if I'm about to be late and there is nothing I can do about it, I move my attention to observe that it is only a minor discomfort in my belly, not to an exaggerated story that being late will lead to embarrassment or perhaps being fired, that I will never find a job again, and that I will probably wind up destitute on the streets. Without the story and the resulting discomfort driving me, I can then make an informed choice: Be late or be late in anguish. Those are my only two choices. And really, given such a stark choice, who would possibly choose the latter? The simple shift in attention helps cut off the self-perpetuating anguish-inducing story and allows me to clearly think through a strategy for dealing with the issue.

Mark McCrea, a mediator who trains on the energetic and ritual dimensions of process, puts it succinctly (paraphrasing Shantideva, an eighth-century Buddhist monk): "If you can't do something, don't worry. If you can do something, don't worry."[11]

Likewise in a room charged with emotion. Many thoughts and stories arise as one is leading or participating in a process. Think about the last meeting you attended or led, for example. As you were tracking whatever was being discussed, did you find yourself being triggered either positively or negatively by something that someone said or did? If the discussion got heated or wildly off track, what did it feel like within your body?

The key skill for these situations is allowing yourself to notice the feeling while still being engaged in the process. That is a focus of many meditative or mindful practices: to learn to observe what is happening within, to "create greater awareness of one's thoughts, emotions, and body sensations by observing them from a witness position without judging them,"[12] while still engaging with the world around you. In Vipassana meditation, for instance, one might reach a meditative state by simply observing the breath, either the air flowing in and out of the tips of your nostrils, or the feeling of your chest rising and falling against your shirt. The point of the practice is not to reach some mystical state of emptiness or holiness; the practice *is* the practice. Simply learning to observe your breath, noticing the thoughts that arise, and gently setting them aside to bring your attention back to your breath develops the ability to observe *whatever* happens inside as you go through your day. You can then gently bring your attention to the task at hand, whatever it is.

Say, for example, a baby starts to cry in the seat behind you in a cramped airplane on a long flight. You might instinctively get agitated and start to play out in your mind just how bad it's likely to get before your flight is over and all the ways it will inevitably feel worse and worse. That agitation will lead to more frustration, leading to more agitation, and so on. You might even start to play out stories in your mind about the parents'

Figure 5.4. *Meditation pond (by Bob Peterson from North Palm Beach, Florida, Planet Earth! [CC BY-SA 2.0, desaturated from the original], via Wikimedia Commons from Wikimedia Commons).*

abilities and how if only they were better parents, none of this would be happening.

Alternately, you could notice the very first signs of agitation in your belly, and instead of allowing it to lead you to greater discomfort, use it as a flag to instead let your attention gently rest on the feeling, just as you learned to pay attention to your breath. As you notice the physical manifestation of the agitation, you can more calmly notice the beginnings of the story you are about to weave, just as you learned to observe your thoughts and gently set them aside. Then you are in a place to make a calm and conscious choice: The baby will cry and you will be agitated, or the baby will cry and you will be empathetic. The practice of observing what is happening within can allow you to more objectively decide which of these you prefer. If you decide the latter, and maybe even offer an encouraging smile to the parents to help take some of the social pressure off them, you will no doubt begin to feel less agitated immediately. In fact, you may notice that the crying itself is really not that bothersome.

Of course, this is not an easy skill to develop; that's why it's called a practice. Like exercise, you have to keep at it regularly to be of any benefit. But, like exercise, it gets easier over time. With practice.

The World Without

As we have discussed before, three of the worlds lie mostly within us: our physical, emotional, and perceptual beings. However, this last one feels like it straddles the internal (the intellectual mind) and the external (the intuitive mind, which seems to tap into deeper and wider knowledge). We have seen how mindfulness can help us escape the internal struggle triggered by a physical response, then taken on by emotional turmoil, and finally reinforced by perceptual stories of anguish. All this feels like it takes place within, yet many facilitators also explicitly draw on the fourth world, the world of spirit, to help with their intrapersonal work.

Jerry Delli Priscoli is a facilitator with the U.S. Army Corps of Engineers who, over the years, has helped the Corps develop their entire approach to conflict prevention and resolution, initially in the United States and increasingly internationally. Corps-related disputes are usually related to big, technical projects, such as dams. Or protecting New Orleans.

So Jerry often deals with roomfuls of pretty irate people with lots at stake. For a sense of the structure he works within, just notice again the name of his institution: Army. Corps. Engineers.

Yet Jerry is devoutly and deeply Catholic. Before every facilitation, he once told me, he comes into the room in advance of the participants and invokes the Holy Spirit to help guide his work.[13] Years ago, Jerry wrote about his faith and mediation:[14]

How is it that those who will not talk, do come to the table? How is that those who previously could see only animosity, create solutions? I say, "I didn't do it. Holy spirit was present." . . . What do we do at the table? We "facilitate." But what is this? We endorse those at table to engage each other in their uniqueness. Isn't that an encounter with God? Isn't that what we do when we facilitate? And isn't that what He did in His Life? Perhaps we bear no more simple but crucial witness than to help each other listen.

Vahid Alavian, whom I mentioned in chapter 1 as being so influential to my own path, worked for the World Bank for more than a decade before moving to serve in the Secretariat of the Bahá'í faith's administrative body at their World Governing Body in Haifa, Israel. While living in Israel, he also acted on behalf of the bank to help negotiate a massive water and energy project between Israel, Jordan, and the Palestinian Authority. The Red–Dead Canal is projected to cost more than $2 billion and would bring water from the Red Sea at Aqaba northward through the Negev Desert, to be dropped for hydropower at the Dead Sea, more than 400 meters below sea level. The problem (besides the technical, environmental, and financial challenges) is that the Jordan River and Dead Sea are shared by all three countries, and relations between them are tenuous, even at the best of times.

Vahid's Bahá'í faith and practices help carry him through discussions such as these, and he regularly calls on divine guidance directly to help him work through challenges and difficulties. He described to me one instance of being answered directly, in the opening phase of discussions over the Red–Dead Canal, paraphrased here:

> The setting was pretty tense, especially between Israelis and Palestinians. At one meeting held in the King David Hotel in Jerusalem, arrival of the Palestinian delegation was delayed because they tried to enter Israel through a check point not designated to allow them through; a different check point for crossing had been agreed by the parties in advance. An official delegation being stopped at a check point is usually a humiliating experience and can be the cause for elevated tension. They finally arrived and, despite the mood, we needed to make progress. I knew if we went right into the agenda and discussions, they would start off badly. One or more parties

may walk out and we might never recover. So, I called for Divine assistance.

Sure enough, I heard what seemed to be a clear voice in my head: "Start with a recess and ask each delegate to find something nice and memorable to say about someone else in the room." There were about twenty-five in the room, twelve delegates plus support staff. Fortunately, and after some initial hesitation, everyone did, and the mood shifted palpably. The Palestinians had brought a long accusatory opening statement that they decided to abandon, an exceedingly generous gesture that helped move us forward.[15]

Although both Jerry and Vahid opened up about the relationship between their spiritual and professional worlds, my experience is that in the West these topics do not arise organically. My suspicion, confirmed only anecdotally, is that their experience is more typical than not.

Sharon Pickett, a mediator from Bethesda, Maryland, describes her preparation for practice in *ACResolution*, a magazine for conflict resolution professionals:

Before beginning a mediation session with clients, I often take a couple of minutes to close my eyes and focus on my breathing. I consciously bring my full awareness into the room and invite my higher self to be present. I remind myself to just be here now and let my own problems go. I want to avoid making judgments and not be invested in the outcome. I remember that I do not know the people sitting with me or understand the life experiences that have shaped who they are. . . . When an impasse occurs I will remember to trust the mediation process and not get anxious. I'll not get so focused on the end agreement that I forget to stay present to the conversation in front of me. I'll strive to create a space where difficult conversations feel safe, and bring my compassion, patience, and wisdom into the room, as well as my intellect. I want to work from that inner place where I can witness what may happen in the mediation without getting hooked by it. I want to let go of my own agenda and radically accept that this is their journey

Figure 5.5. *A quiet moment (photo by Capitol Standard, https://unsplash .com/@lauristonu [CC0]).*

and remember that I am only a guide to help them stay on the path they choose to take. I'm grateful for the opportunity to do this work and welcome these people into my life for the next two hours. Then I open my eyes, and greet my clients with a smile and a peaceful heart.[16]

Back to Tbilisi

Recall from the beginning of this chapter my meeting in Tbilisi, Georgia, where one of the delegates was pretty irate and focused his frustration full bore on me in Russian. After about 5 minutes of yelling at me with great gusto and pace, he suddenly stopped, really quite abruptly. He had thrown down his challenge to me and now needed me to respond. Having put forward that much anger with that much energy, his body language in that pause showed that he was quite expecting an extremely energetic answer from me in response, either angry or defensive. And I quite possibly might have gone that route—I was pretty clearly attacked personally and professionally—and I could easily have let my defense mechanism lead to a vociferous response.

Except for two things.

The first was that by then, I had worked with mindful practices just enough to be able to track what was happening inside and to use my observation to help craft a path that would not be led by my defensiveness. I certainly felt the beginnings of a physical trigger as the delegate was yelling. A discomfort started to gnaw in the pit of my stomach, and I felt my body's fight-or-flight mechanism come alive. My breathing started to quicken, and my muscles began to tense. In my sharpening peripheral vision, I took in the attention that all the participants and my colleagues were paying to me, waiting to see what my response would be. And I scripted the very beginnings of a story in my head about how all of this was unfair, how I had flown umpteen hours to be here to help, how my role was being undermined, and how I would never recover.

But then the mindfulness training kicked in. I allowed myself to simply observe my physical response to the situation, and I was able to start to really separate out my observations of my internal workings with the workings themselves. Although this played out in only a second or two, it felt much, much longer. Sure enough, I felt decreasingly led by the turmoil that my physical, emotional, and perceptual beings were creating for each other, and I could then gently shift my attention to more clearly focus on the delegate and his intentions.

As I listened to the delegate rage and could focus more on him and less on me, I tried really hard to listen for what exactly had triggered his ire. What was the vulnerability that he was trying to protect with his anger?

But I said that there were two things that helped de-escalate the situation and, if truth be told, it was the second that had more immediate impacts. Quite simply, the interpreter could not keep up. As the delegate's pace increased, the interpreter fell further and further behind. So when the delegate finally stopped and clearly needed an immediate response to satisfy him, the room instead was filled with a really, really awkward silence. In that silence, I signaled to him helplessly, pointing to my headset as I continued to listen to the last minutes of his tirade from the interpreter.

It was such an awkward moment—his spent anger, my helplessness, the interpreter's furious catching up, and the single space that required a response that just was not forthcoming—that the room erupted into laughter. And the delegate, angry though he was, finally looked around at the ludicrousness of it all and started to chuckle himself.

By then the moment had passed, and once the interpreter had caught up, it was easy for me to let the delegate know that this was the way I started most processes, that there was nothing special about this group, and by choosing these ice breakers I certainly was not motivated by any preconceptions of these particular delegates. I asked him to give me the rest of the day, and that we could discuss any change of course over dinner if necessary. Kindly, he agreed, and we proceeded through the day productively.

So what was the issue? What had so triggered the delegate?

Fortunately, the whole group was scheduled to go out to a welcome dinner together that night, a huge event formally hosted by the government of Georgia. And at dinner, a custom of the Caucasus kicked in, that of the toastmaster's special role. As in many parts of the world at a formal dinner, one person is designated to find something nice to say about every person in the room in order. And, in the Caucasus, each toast is followed by a shot of vodka.

There were seventeen of us in the room.

I happened to be sitting across from the once-irate delegate, and, as the toastmaster led us through the magnificent attributes and heroic qualities of delegate after delegate, our relationship got warmer and warmer. We exchanged friendly toasts ourselves, taught each other celebratory songs, and exchanged pictures of our children.

Finally, I was able to ask, albeit a bit obliquely, what had gotten him so angry. In the long, circuitous story he told me about his history and that of his country, the landmine I had stepped on became clear.

When the Caucasus were part of the Soviet Union, scientists and resource managers from the region were treated with tremendous respect, both within the country and at international meetings. They were, after all, the cream of the cream—cutting-edge, world-class professionals—and much of the world looked to them for their expertise. When the Soviet Union fell apart, the only thing that really changed for them was the economy. They were still just as smart and just as accomplished, but suddenly members of the international community no longer came to learn but to "help."

Those who have been the recipients of charity know what a blow it can be to one's self-esteem, and thus it was even at a national level. The delegate told withering stories of aid agencies showing up to help him and his colleagues learn to wash their hands. "I have a PhD in biochemistry!" he exclaimed.

And so my role-playing exercises inadvertently poured salt on a particularly gaping wound in that particular part of the world at that particular time. The exercises were seen as condescending in a region whose collective self-esteem was already badly bruised.

When I work internationally, I generally try to team up with a local facilitator precisely for this reason: One never understands all the political nuance and sensitivities of a region, and a poorly informed facilitator can do more harm than good without such understanding. I had teamed up here too, but both my partner and I had just missed this one.

The next day (speaking softly because of our collective headache), I made a point of mentioning that I used the interactive exercises wherever I worked, and at all levels, from ministers on down—that it was just something I generally found useful—and we were able to move forward quite productively. The formerly angry delegate, my new friend, helped lead the exercises with gusto.

~

Meditation and prayer may not seem the most intuitive tools for a facilitator, but they can be immensely powerful. And, truth be told, every now and again a bit of vodka doesn't hurt either.

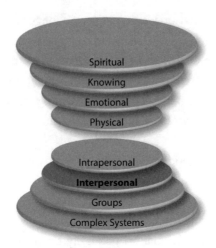

Figure 6.1.

Table 6.1
Four Needs and Their Expressions

Four Worlds and Foundational Needs	Four Expressions: Pursuit of Needs in Dialogue and Negotiations
Physical	Positions
Emotional	Interests
Perceptual	Values
Spiritual	Harmony

CHAPTER SIX

Listening with the Heart: Transforming Interpersonal Conflict

Silence illuminates our souls,
whispers to our hearts,
and brings them together. —*Kahlil Gibran*

Lenin could listen so intently that he exhausted the speaker.
  —*Sir Isaiah Berlin*

Q: For an American, what's the opposite of speaking?
A: Waiting to speak. —*Joke heard overseas*

The Balcony and the Mekong Spirit

The Mekong River Commission (MRC) has been in existence since 1957, with initial support from the United States as a way to use infrastructure development activity as a bastion against communism. The thinking went as follows: Help the countries develop their water resources as we have done in the western United States, and the Soviet Union and China will have less appeal to the four countries of the Lower Mekong: Laos, Vietnam, Thailand, and Cambodia.

Although the priorities and incentives have shifted dramatically over the years, along with regional geopolitics, the MRC has survived, as have dialogue and information sharing throughout the tumult of ensuing decades. One plan that did not materialize because of the turmoil, however, was a cascade of eighteen main stem dams that was envisioned for the river by the U.S. Bureau of Reclamation at the MRC's inception. Although hydropower development at such a scale may have provided power for much of Southeast Asia and perhaps fueled economic growth throughout the region, it also would have decimated fisheries, ecosystems, and local communities all along the river and beyond.

In fact, it is only recently that main stem dams are being proposed and implemented, mostly by Laos, as one of the few resources that can help move the country out of least-developed status. But new awareness of the potential harm that such projects can cause to both people and the environment, along with greater political clout carried by opposing forces, have created a difficult setting for discussion.

A number of years ago, I was helping to facilitate discussions in the region about transboundary environmental impact assessments, that is, how countries monitor, inform, and compensate each other for pollutants and other environmental impacts that cross international boundaries. Generally in the region, although the issues are tense, culture often dictates that conflicts are not expressed directly and almost never explosively.

Working in Southeast Asia as a Western-trained facilitator gives one a front-row experience of the Enlightenment Rift. Direct discussion of conflict is often considered rude, and in some circles, showing anger is seen as a mental disorder.[1] Other Westerners have expressed frustration that conflicts are not dealt with directly, making the process seemingly more difficult and definitely lengthier.[2] In contrast, Diana Suhardiman, a European-trained engineer and social scientist originally from Indonesia, and currently with the International Water Management Institute in Laos, explained the view from her perspective: "In the East, an individual does not exist without their community. It's not that we are avoiding conflict. It's that we are working really hard to retain harmony."[3]

The predominance of group or community over individual is not an abstract philosophy but is carried through in all moments of one's life. A trivial but telling example: Often in ice breakers, I use a game that involves a simulation of arm wrestling, where pairs of participants start by competing against each other before the exercise evolves to more of a cooperative game. It is brief and evocative, and it usually breaks some

Figure 6.2. *Tai chi exercises near Elephant Trunk Hill in Guilin, China (by Dennis Jarvis from Halifax, Canada [China-7852 (CC BY-SA 2.0), via Wikimedia Commons from Wikimedia Commons]).*

initial tensions inherent in most groups with which I work. Over the years I have learned about, and then learned to work around, cultural barriers to the game (teaming up pairs by gender or professional hierarchy where mixing is inappropriate, for example) and the game has worked well just about worldwide.

The first time I tried it in Southeast Asia, though, I could tell this was a profoundly new setting for me. There were no problems as I paired participants up and explained the rules. But when I said, "Go!" to mark the first 10 seconds of arm wrestling, no one moved. Each pair sat across from each other, grasping hands on their tables in classic arm wrestling posture, but neither applied any pressure at all. None.

As I have mentioned, when I work internationally, I always work with a local partner to help us through regional nuance. As I watched the lengthening inaction in the room, I sidled up to Dr. Vitoon Viriyasakultorn, my partner and a world-class facilitator based in Bangkok.

"What's going on?" I asked. "Did they understand the rules?"

"Sure, they know how to arm wrestle."

"Well, why aren't they moving?

"It's a question of honor."

"So you're saying no one wants to lose? That would be dishonorable. Is that it?"

"No, the opposite. No one wants to win. That would cause their opponent to lose face."

~

These discussions on cross-border environmental impacts on the Mekong were a little different, though. Each of the four Lower Mekong countries was represented by a small team of technical and policy experts, and I had tried to craft a fairly informal setting despite the formalities of the issues. As ever, the meeting was in a nondescript set of government offices, although we did have the benefit of one entire wall almost entirely of glass: large windows that led to a small balcony overlooking a lush and fragrant garden from our second floor.

As I have mentioned before, there often is a tangible energy in a room, and here there was palpable discord even before we started the dialogue, centered on one of the delegates. This surprised me a bit, because the issues seemed on the surface to be pretty technical and not tied directly to any of the more sensitive topics that exist between the countries.

But there is a truism in facilitation that "the issue is never the issue," so I proceeded with caution.

Sure enough, as soon as the first seemingly trivial proposal was put forward, it was immediately and loudly quashed by the one country representative whose discordant energy I had noticed. Same with the second. And the third. In fact, this delegate was apparently opposed to everything that the rest of the group thought, even the suggested time for the lunch break.

With each proposal, the delegate became more emphatic and angrier, resulting in the rest of the room becoming more and more frustrated at the lack of even trivial progress.

William Ury, one of ADR's senior statesmen and co-author of the classic *Getting to Yes*, followed that book with one titled, naturally, *Getting Past*

Figure 6.3. Pavilion balcony overlooking Hakone Gardens, Saratoga, California *(by Daderot [Own work] [Public domain], via Wikimedia Commons from Wikimedia Commons).*

No.[4] In it, he uses a descriptive allusion for how to circumvent such precarious impasses: "Don't react. Go to the balcony," he suggests. Although he meant it metaphorically, alluding to the larger and more objective view afforded from a higher, more removed vantage, we actually did have a balcony, and its little oasis of verdant quiet hearkened.

Calling a break, I asked the agitated delegate to take a walk outside with me.

"How's it going?" I asked.

"How's it going??!! How can you even ask that??!! Don't you see what those people are doing? How they're taking advantage of us? Bullying us?"

And that was just the beginning. In the ensuing tirade, every sentence started with "them" or "those people," and how they were out of line in so, so many ways.

Over the years, as I've said, one of the things I've learned is that the issue is almost never the issue. And the only way to figure out what really is going on is to listen. Really listen. With the heart.

The Four Worlds and the Other in the Mirror

As we broaden our framework from potential internal discord in the previous chapter to interpersonal dialogue in this, we begin, as ever, with the four worlds. One key addition to consider as we interact with others is our innate and profound instinct to protect our core physical, emotional, perceptual, and spiritual needs. Twentieth-century scholars and practitioners such as Abraham Maslow and Marshall Rosenberg have described these key needs and the psychological and emotional challenges that result when they are threatened.[5] In *Emotional Intelligence*, Daniel Goleman[6] coined the term "amygdala hijack" to describe how the instinctive brain overrides the thinking brain with urgent choices to fight or flee when one is seemingly threatened.

As ever, the roots of these wisdoms are much more ancient.[7]

Most faith traditions describe a concept of individuals and their relationship to divine energy or flow, sometimes referred to as grace, and the theological and psychological impacts of aligning oneself and one's actions with that flow, or the discord that results from nonalignment.

Figure 6.4. Light from Heaven *(painting by Orit Martin, website: www
.oritmartin.com; used with permission).*

In Kabbalistic terms, for example, one might imagine the *sfirot* of the
Tree of Life—emanations of divine attributes that we saw in chapter 4—
almost as a series of conduits for the flow of grace from the transcendent,
holy world above to our mundane, profane world below. Conversely, the
image could represent the flow of our intents and actions working either to increase or decrease that flow from this seemingly profane world.
Within this construct, our goal in this lifetime is to do what we can to enhance the flow of grace, by essentially "aligning our will with God's will"
to help repair this world and work to uncover the profane garments that
hide the holiness inherent throughout the entire universe.[8]

As guidance for how to practically do this work, Jews draw 613 specific

BOX 6.1

ATTRIBUTES OF DIVINE MERCY FROM EXODUS 34:6–7[a]
PARAMITAS (TRANSCENDENTAL ACTIONS)
TO OVERCOME THE THREE POISONS[b]

1 *Adonai:* compassion before a person sins;

2 *Adonai:* compassion after a person has sinned;

3 *El:* mighty in compassion to give all creatures according to their need;

4 *Rachum:* merciful, that humankind may not be distressed;

5 *VeChanun:* and gracious if humankind is already in distress;

6 *Erech appayim:* slow to anger;

7 *VeRav chesed:* and plenteous in kindness;

8 *VeEmet:* and truth;

9 *Notzer chesed laalafim:* keeping kindness unto thousands;

10 *Noseh avon:* forgiving iniquity;

11 *VaFeshah:* and transgression;

12 *VeChata'ah:* and sin;

13 *VeNakeh:* and pardoning.

- *Dāna pāramī:* generosity, giving of oneself
- *Sīla pāramī:* virtue, morality, proper conduct
- *Nekkhamma pāramī:* renunciation
- *Paññā pāramī:* transcendental wisdom, insight
- *Viriya pāramī:* energy, diligence, vigor, effort
- *Khanti pāramī:* patience, tolerance, forbearance, acceptance, endurance
- *Sacca pāramī:* truthfulness, honesty
- *Adhiṭṭhāna pāramī:* determination, resolution
- *Mettā pāramī:* lovingkindness
- *Upekkhā pāramī:* equanimity, serenity

a. *Enumeration and English translation from Isidore Singer, ed.,* The Jewish Encyclopedia *(New York: Funk & Wagnalls, 1904), 546.*

b. *Six come from the Mahayana tradition, and Theravada adds four more. From Sulak Sivaraksa,* Conflict, Culture, Change: Engaged Buddhism in a Globalizing World *(Boston: Wisdom Publications, 2005), 4.*

instructions from the Torah to help guide them through their lives. More directly, there are thirteen divine attributes of mercy revealed to Moses on Sinai by which God is said to sustain the world. Although the attributes are of God, as experienced by Moses, they are offered to humanity to emulate for a life of holiness as well.

The concept of seeking alignment with divine flow as humanity's goal would be very familiar to most of Christianity's views on grace, central to church teachings from the Catholic and Eastern churches through the Reformation and to more recent theologies, including the Church of Jesus Christ of Latter-Day Saints.[9] (I am fully aware of how fraught and reductionist a sentence like the previous one is, ignoring vast theologic and historic grappling with both the concept of grace and the relationship between grace and works. For our purposes, though, the main tenet of alignment with a divine flow, and the consequences of divergence from that flow, are all that is needed for the work at hand.)

Although most Buddhist theology does not refer to divinity as a source (being, well, agnostic on the topic), the discord that comes from misalignment from *Dhamma* (Pali, literally, "that which supports," understood as "the Truth within us"[10]) is a central tenet and described as the source of all suffering (*dukkha*).[11] We grasp for things we perceive as pleasurable, avoid things that are not, and generally do not recognize the overall impermanence of both. With this understanding of our desire to continuously retain the pleasurable and avoid the unpleasurable, similar in Hindu and Buddhist constructs, conflict and anger are reactions to change, a consequence of our attachment to the perception of permanence.[12]

The Source of Anger: Within

In each faith tradition, as we move further out of alignment, the internal becomes external, and the result can be anger, conflict, and violence. In Buddhism, taken to an extreme, attraction becomes grasping becomes greed. Avoidance becomes repulsion becomes hatred. And ignorance (of the truth) becomes delusion.

> He [the Buddha] posited that every action originates in the mind and is then expressed through either speech or a bodily act. . . . This mental violence is of three types: greed, hatred, and delusion or ignorance, known as the Three Poisons.[13]

Similarly in the Kabbalistic model, the source of anger and even evil starts internally. Recall our balance of three divine attributes from chapter 2 of *din* (justice), *chesed* (mercy), and *rachamim* (compassion). Recall too that this balance is understood as part of a map of the universe (actually

Balance in Conflict

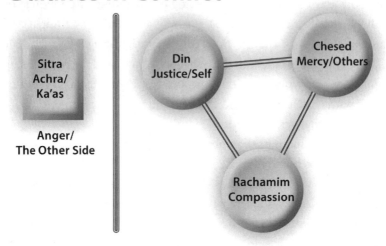

Figure 6.5.

of God's consciousness, which, in this theology, is essentially the same thing) and, because we are created in the divine image, a map of our consciousness as well. One can think of left brain (self, rational, bounded, rule-oriented, past-remembering, and future-planning) balanced by right brain (other, expansive, loving, spiritual, connected, and present in the moment). And both sit in a balance expressed by and led from the heart.[14]

In this model, the source of anger is portrayed as out of alignment on the far left side—the *sitra achra*, in Aramaic literally, "the other side"—our bounded-ness taken to the extreme. Quite literally, then, the source of anger is too much self.[15]

And this makes a lot of sense in a conflict management context as well. Anger at others starts internally, with a story about how right we are about something.[16] Our bounded nature is perceived as being under attack; one or several of our internal four basic needs (physical, emotional, perceptual, or spiritual) is being threatened, and we feel vulnerable. If we continue to stew or if the threat continues, our *rightness* becomes *righteousness* and, finally, *self-righteousness*, until we are so self-righteous in our anger we can do harm to others.[17]

In *Sha'arei Orah*, Joseph ben Abraham Gikatilla's (1248–c. 1305) classic

---

BOX 6.2

TAKEAWAY SKILLS

- Anger is a shield protecting vulnerability.
- Therefore, the source of anger is internal, not external.
- Alleviating our own anger starts with a focus on our own vulnerability rather than on the external trigger.
- The most productive way to meet anger in others is to listen, deeply listen, for the source, and only then enter into dialogue.

---

work of the Kabbalah, he metaphorically describes this process as a trial held in the heavenly realm, where Justice and Lovingkindness each have their say, and Compassion makes a decision, which is carried out in this physical plane (*malchut*). If the decision is negative, the worlds above and below are separated, leaving the world below alone with *sitra achra*, the "other side," resulting in hatred, despair, and destruction.[18] This feels like a powerful allusion to our internal workings as our higher and lower selves struggle with each other, moderated by our heart's intuition, as well as to similar struggles at the societal level.

The Four Worlds and Their Expressions in Process

Although the trigger or irritant to our vulnerabilities may be outside us, then, the entire process begins within and can become exacerbated to the point where we can do real damage, either internally or externally.

Think about the most contentious issues of the day from the understanding that anger is a shield protecting vulnerability, and we can fairly readily identify which of the four worlds is perceived as being threatened. In issues of gun control in the United States, for example, both sides feel unsafe; their physical safety feels profoundly threatened.

"I feel so unsafe; I want fewer guns on the streets."

"I feel so unsafe; I want more guns around me for protection."

Or climate change, where the intellectual underpinnings of both sides are challenged:

"How can they ignore the overwhelming data? They are being manipulated by the right."

BOX 6.3

EXERCISE

Think deeply about most of the issues that trigger your own ire, and see
whether you can identify the internal need that is being threatened, whether
physical, emotional, perceptual, or spiritual. (Please do not use issues that are
the result of any real trauma in your life or in the lives of your loved ones.)

- When somebody cuts into your line in traffic far ahead of you while you
  are waiting patiently, does that irk you? Why, when it does not threaten
  your physical safety? Is it more an emotional sense of justice? Do you feel
  you are following the rules and so should others?
- Think of a political position that really bothers you and try to figure out
  why. Instead of trying to analyze the views of proponents that you feel are
  misguided, check in with your internal trigger. Is it a perceptual threat?
  Meaning, is it threatening the way you see the world? A physical threat to
  current or future generations?
- Are there issues of faith or secularism that are irksome to you, even anger-
  ing? What is threatened in your own spiritual worldview by the issue?

"How can they manipulate the data so overwhelmingly? They are being used by the left."

To develop strategies for dealing with these internal sparks, it is worth
thinking about how the four worlds express themselves in our interactions with others. Table 6.2 shows the four worlds and a parallel flow
of how protecting those needs is manifested in dialogue or negotiations,
whether formal or informal, in four expressions:

These *expressions* are how our needs are expressed in dialogue. They
parallel the four worlds in that they move ever deeper from the most basic
and apparent (or upward, if that is easier to picture; as we saw earlier, the
concepts "higher" and "deeper" converge in these constructs) to more
ephemeral and inclusive. Like the four worlds, as we move deeper (or
higher), distinctions dissipate, and we tend to find more commonality.

In essence, *positions* is *what* somebody wants. In my world, the "what"
is generally more water. *Interests* is *why* they want it (to irrigate, move
barges, generate hydropower, or protect the environment, for example).
One major contribution of alternative dispute resolution, from *Getting to
Yes* onward, is the centrality of "interest-based" bargaining that suggests,

---

BOX 6.4

TAKEAWAY SKILLS

In general, there are three triggers to anger, all internal:

- One's physical, emotional, perceptual, and/or spiritual needs are threatened, as described in this chapter.
- One feels that someone else has broken a social contract that one voluntarily follows (e.g., cut in line).
- One reacts to traits of others that reflect those that bother us about ourselves. (If it irks you especially when people talk loudly or cut into your sentences, for example, check in to see whether these are things you do to others.)

On this last point, the Baal Shem Tov, the founder of the Chassidic movement, taught the theological reason for this: Inasmuch as people are generally in denial, they may be unaware of their own character defects.

Therefore, God shows them their character defects in another person, where they are easier to identify and address. "The world is a mirror," the Baal Shem Tov said. "The faults you see in others are your own."[a]

Regardless, when something starts to bother you, try to reframe the issue from "Why does *that* bother me?," which is a question about the external stimulus, to "Why does that bother *me*?," a question about internal vulnerability.[b]

a. Nechoma Greisman, "Noach: Looking at Yourself Through Others," ed. Rabbi Moshe Miller (Chabad.org http://www.chabad.org/library/article_cdo/aid/97527/jewish/Noach-Looking-at-Yourself-Through -Others.htm).

b. It should go without saying that if someone is being tangibly threatened, the first response should be to protect oneself however possible. These exercises are for sources of anger not rooted in crises, trauma, or actual threats.

Table 6.2
Four Worlds and Four Expressions

Four Internal Needs	Four Expressions of Needs in Negotiations
Physical	Positions
Emotional	Interests
Perceptual	Values
Spiritual	Harmony

rightly, that working from positions alone often is a zero-sum game; one side's gain is another side's loss. There is only so much water, so position-based dialogue can be seen as pitting farms against the environment, for instance. If we go a bit deeper to interests, though, we might find some nuance in the issues that allow all needs to be met. A farm upstream might be cooperatively managed in consideration of a fragile wetland downstream, allowing water for both growing crops and sustaining the wetland at sensitive times.

Values is a deeper level yet and begins to tap broader ethical guidelines that we each have at our core. Values center on our four basic needs—physical, emotional, perceptual, and spiritual—and people on seemingly opposite sides of an issue often find that they share basic values. Farmers and environmentalists generally appreciate both healthy environments and healthy economies. Almost everyone wants good schools, functioning governments, safe neighborhoods, and solid health care, and they differ only on the means (positions) to get there.

The last of the expressions is *harmony*,[19] where, as musically (or spiritually), each individual note is represented in a melodious whole. Although this is an aspirational goal of many dialogues, it is really, really hard to achieve. Just as the perceptual state straddles the internal and the external, however, often working from the expression of values can slide into the realm of harmony. So for our purposes, having values lead a dialogue, as discussed below, can help achieve a level of harmony between individuals or within a community.

Here are some examples of the four expressions:

A hypothetical rancher and environmentalist are having a discussion about a limited water supply. The *positions*—the "what"—are that each side wants more water. The *interests*—the "why"—are that one wants to water their animals and crops and the other wants water instream for fish and the aquatic ecosystem. The *values* might be that one is living out a lifestyle carried on for generations or, more pragmatically, they might see themselves as contributing to the food supply of a hungry world. The other is protecting an intricate and fragile web of life either for its own sake or for the sake of those who depend on it for lives or livelihoods. *Harmony* might come if we delved deep enough into beliefs and motiva-

Figure 6.6. *Riverbank restoration project, eastern Oregon (photo courtesy of the author).*

tion: Perhaps both see themselves as contributing to a larger design and protecting fragile systems, both human and nonhuman.

The key here is that, similar to the four worlds, as we get deeper in these "four expressions," distinctions between us start to dissipate, as we delve deeper from *positions* (what people want), *interests* (why they want it), and finally to *values* (the core on which their interests are based) and *harmony* (the underlying unity of the universe). Because differences can dissipate the deeper one goes, and because harmony can be so elusive, there are practitioners who increasingly advocate value-led, rather than interest-based, dialogue.

"Values-based decision making," for example, is an increasingly popular term in dispute management and in group processes in, for example, health care and business. Although values are difficult to define, even in the business context, it is difficult to talk about them without bordering on the spiritual. Dianne Hall and colleagues[20] describe the core values exhibited by "types of men" from E. Spranger[21] (theoretical, social, political, religious, aesthetic, and economic) and how these concepts become secularized in J. F. Courtney's[22] decision-making paradigm (technical, organizational, personal, ethical, and aesthetic). More recently, Richard Barrett, a leader in business strategic training, defined values as "the energetic containers of our aspirations and intentions."[23] Mindtools.com lists more than one hundred core values, and offers exercises for how to identify one's own. For our purposes, of course, I would define our values as the concepts that protect and sustain our four basic sets of needs, as we will discuss later in the chapter.

Starting a conversation at the values level, rather than interests or positions, can start where we have commonality, then ease us "backwards" into the more contentious issues. But getting there *after* we establish what we have in common can make the subsequent conversation a bit less fraught.

At a recent meeting on very contentious dams in Southeast Asia, representatives from the pro-dam and anti-dam forces were guided in an exchange that exemplified this point. At its essence, the dialogue went as follows:

"What is your position on the proposed dam?"

Pro: "I am for it."

Anti: "I am against it."

"Why do you have the position that you have?"

Pro: "I am worried about poverty, and I think the dam will help alleviate it."

Anti: "I am worried about the environment, and I think the dam will damage it."

"And on what core values do you base your beliefs?"

Pro: "I love my country."

Anti: "I love my country."

And then we had an entry point for dialogue.

Starting a conversation at values helps profoundly in another skill advocated by practitioners: the art of reframing. Deborah Shmueli, a geographer at Haifa University, and her colleagues[24] describe how the frames people use to give context to issues can dramatically increase the intractability of differences:

BOX 6.5

FINDING OUR COMMON VALUES EXERCISE

For this role-play exercise, you will need another person, perhaps a friend or, if you are feeling brave, someone with whom you have substantive disagreements. Ideally, these would be political and not personal differences (and as ever, definitely not something that alludes to any real crisis or trauma).

The exercise is this: Identify two diametrically opposing roles of either real or imaginary people who viscerally disagree over some hot-button issue of the day, maybe First or Second Amendment rights, for example, or some topic of the far left versus the far right.

Identify which of you will play which role. It doesn't matter whether you believe in the viewpoint you are representing; this is a role play.

Now in role, see whether you can identify three things on which you agree. Now switch roles and see whether you can find three more. Most people find this much easier to do than they would have thought. Our political discourse and social media tend to emphasize our differences to the point that we often forget just how much we have in common.

If you have been truthful and thoughtful, you now have a list of six core values, any of which would be a great place to start a conversation.

Frame divergence often contributes to the intractability of conflicts. Disputants differ not only in interests, beliefs, and values but also in how they perceive the situation at the conscious and preconscious levels.[25]

Working from values allows the complexity of a problem to remain yet opens a path to reframe the problem from a place of commonality. Writing about complex resource conflicts, my colleague and friend Julia Doermann, a senior water policy advisor for agencies and governments throughout the U.S. West, has noted that we often assume the problem that is presented is the problem to be solved.[26] It is also common to stay with familiar framing because entering into an inquiry about highly complex, dynamic challenges seems fruitless. We assume that people can't work together in the face of different political beliefs, economic pressures, scarcity of the resource, and cultural differences. We think that keeping it simple will get us to a resolution quicker:

For conflicts that chronically occur or are part of a larger, systemic pattern of conflicts, we need to examine the framing of the problem. While simplistic framing is tempting, holistic framing may be necessary to make any real progress.

Reframing a problem is an art that can be cultivated. It requires being able to track to the root of a problem and not get distracted by the symptoms.[27]

Julia describes how "mythic stories" that we have about ourselves are expressions of our values and how homing in on them helps us find common ground:

At a forum among farmers, ranchers, the timber industry, environmentalists, public servants from local, state, federal, and tribal governments, each spoke from their position about non–point source water pollution and its contribution to the decline of wild salmon. Their stories all sounded different on their face. Many felt challenged and misunderstood by the others, which led to tension and conflict in the room. Some got quiet and folded their arms—but in fury and defensiveness. Others expressed frustrations with some of the others with rather aggressive projections.

In the end, however, it was possible to sort out that there was a difference between the practices and the mythic stories. *All were expressing the same mythic story about themselves. They all saw themselves as stewards of the land and environment; the practices were what differed.* They could then see their common goals, and focus their attention on what were acceptable practices to meet their common goals, and how would they achieve this collectively.[28] (italics added)

Getting to values can take quite a bit of work as we delve deeper and deeper. One helpful tool in reframing is to allow the structure of our language to reflect the deeper levels where distinctions start to dissipate. A classic exercise that does this is to turn *ors* into *ands*:

"Shall we develop the economy *or* protect the environment?" becomes "How can we development the economy *and* protect the environment?"

"Shall we build the dam *or* have healthy farms?" becomes "How can we build a dam *and* have healthy farms?"

***Figure 6.7.** Stakeholder workshop in the Mekong River basin (photo courtesy of the author).*

Another tool to use to facilitate a value-driven discussion is to add the concept of sustainability in framing the problem. Oregon's past governor John Kitzhaber, a former emergency room physician who was elected to an unprecedented four terms and who was responsible for elaborate environmental policies, followed classic definitions to describe sustainability as "managing the use, development and protection of our economic, environmental, and community resources in a way and at a rate that enables people to meet their current needs without compromising the ability of future generations to do the same."

In his policy work, he advocated for reframing complex problems to get to shared values by including sustainability, an approach he termed "enlibra." He argued that the three components of sustainability, what others have called the "triple bottom line"—environmental, economic, and social sustainability—*are* our shared values. (Of course, as I noted earlier, I would argue adding sustainability of a fourth, spiritual dimension, getting us back to the four worlds—the first three being our physical environment, the emotional security of a healthy social system, and the "knowing" approach to a healthy economy.) He laid out the premise in more detail in a 2002 speech and gave examples for reframing using sustainability:

> I would suggest to you that the debate over logging old growth may well fall into the same category. Isn't the real economic issue involved here how to maintain a sustainable supply of timber to our mills—not whether the logs are 80 years old or 300 years old?

BOX 6.6

TAKEAWAY SKILLS

To reframe a problem around shared values:

- Turn *ors* into *ands*.
- Add the concept of sustainability.

BOX 6.7

EXERCISE

Try your hand at reframing with a current natural resource or other issue you are familiar with.

1. Describe how it is framed by those involved.
2. Practice reframing.

The following pointers will help you create a new frame for the complex problem you are dealing with:

1. Replace *ors* with *ands*.
2. Listen for identities and a common mythic story that express values. Describe a vision that everyone can see themselves within.
3. Consider introducing the four components of sustainability—environmental, social, economic, and spiritual—to the story. Perhaps use terms such as *health*, *quality*, or *restoration of systems*.
4. Think in multiple timeframes: Frame in ways that speak to short-term response as well as mid- to long-term strategies for change. Terms that encompass such a time horizon may include words such as *sustainable*.

Source: Modified from Julia Doermann and Aaron T. Wolf, "Western Water Participant Workbook," Sharing Water, Building Relations: Managing and Transforming Water Conflict in the US West. (Denver: U.S. Department of the Interior Bureau of Reclamation, 2012), 113; online at http://www.transbound arywaters.orst.edu/research/US%20Western%20Water/Western%20Water%20Participant%20Work book%202012.pdf.

In my own profession—medicine—we often confuse the debate over access to health care with the challenge of keeping people healthy. Health care is a means to that end—it is not an end in itself. Health care has no intrinsic value beyond its relationship to health. Reframing the debate in this way allows us to ask the real question: what is the value of the health care we are paying for in terms of the health it produces?[29]

Lev Shome'ah: A Listening Heart

[Legendary Columbia University professor] Mark [Van Doren] would come into the room and, without any fuss, would start talking about whatever was to be talked about. Most of the time he asked questions. His questions were very good, and if you tried to answer them intelligently, you found yourself saying excellent things that you did not know you knew, and that you had not, in fact, known before. He had "educed" them from you by his question.

—Thomas Merton, *The Seven Story Mountain*

Thus far in this chapter, we have discussed three key points to how we interact as individuals in conflict:

1. There is inherent discord in nonalignment with _____ (fill in the blank with whichever concept you are most comfortable: grace, divine will, truth, life force, universal energy).

2. The source of ire, agitation, and anger is internal, generally a shield protecting a perceived threat to one's basic needs.

3. Entering and centering a dialogue where we have some commonality (ideally at the level of harmony but more practically at the level of values) is fundamental to finding a way through our differences.

Because both the source of discord and the keys to dialogue are within, we need a tool to help illuminate the inner realms of our partners in dialogue, and that tool is *listening*.

A word about words. The English word *listen* evokes something mechanical that we do with our ears alone, and this is profoundly not what we're after here. Better would be the word *grok*, a term the science fiction writer Robert Heinlein had to make up for his 1961 *Stranger in a Strange Land*, precisely because English has nothing to describe the way Valentine Michael Smith, his Martian-raised protagonist, explains Martian relations with each other and with their environment:

Grok means to understand so thoroughly that the observer becomes a part of the observed—to merge, blend, intermarry, lose identity in group experience. It means almost everything that we mean by religion, philosophy, and science—and it means as little to us (because of our Earthling assumptions) as color means to a blind man.[30]

Perhaps because of a need for such a concept in English, *grok* has actually made it into the Merriam-Webster dictionary, where it is defined as, "to understand profoundly and intuitively."[31]

Had Hebrew been spoken on Mars, Smith might instead have used the term *sh'ma*, a central tenet of Judaism mistranslated to English as "listen" or "hear." To get at what *sh'ma* actually means, we look to its usage in Exodus 24:7, where the Children of Israel accept the obligations of the Torah that Moses is about to bring them[32] with the phrase *"Na'aseh ve'nishma"*— "We will do and we will hear." But not "hear" with our ears; rather, understand it at the core essence of our being. The lesson is that something as deeply powerful as the word of the divine, and all the detailed and nuanced guidelines that provide a container for alignment, cannot be understood simply through technical listening. Something as potent as a path to spirituality can only be understood at its core by doing. In the words of Enzo Bianchi, a Catholic theologian who explains the biblical phrase, "They will live out God's word, and as they do so they will really hear and understand it."[33]

Think about something as seemingly simple as meditation. No matter how much someone says, "Just pay attention to your breath," or no matter how many tomes one reads on the topic, you won't get it until you do it. And do it often, as a practice.

That's *sh'ma*: really and truly getting something (or someone) at the core. And that's the kind of listening we're after. In Sanskrit, the term *shravana* gets us close: It is a listening that recognizes sound as the link to the universal life force, and is described as "listening from depth for depth."[34]

In English, this type of listening always has a modifier. Vietnamese Buddhist monk Thich Nhat Hanh[35] uses the term "deep listening," Andrea Cohen and her colleagues[36] and others refer to "compassionate listening," and Barbara Breitman[37] calls it "contemplative" or "holy" listening. Whatever it is called, its power for connection and healing is unassailable.

Figure 6.8. *Conversation, Essaouira (by gripso_banana_prune [CC BY-SA 2.0, desaturated from the original], via https://www.flickr.com/photos/antony stanley/).*

And where does this kind of listening take place? King Solomon intuits the answer when, instead of asking God for fame or riches he asks for a *lev shome'ah*, a heart that listens.[38]

Recall again our three-sphered Kabbalistic model of left brain (justice) with right brain (lovingkindness) held in perpetual balance and led by the heart (compassion). The *lev shome'ah* is the heart that takes understanding from the ears and the brain and really and truly intuits the meaning, motivations, and context of the other. As Cohen and colleagues put it, "Compassionate Listening is a practice that integrates cognitive awareness with the wisdom of the heart."[39]

The kind of listening we are after has been described in the transcendence of conversations either between us and God or between God and us. In *Lectio Divina* (divine reading), Enzo Bianchi[40] writes an entire chapter on listening as central to a relationship with the divine:

If we want our time spent with the Bible to be productive, we need to listen intensely, with a "listening heart." The entire Bible is predicated on the fact that God speaks and people listen. People in the Bible walk by faith and not by sight, because listening is the only way to an encounter with the living God. . . . The command to listen is central in both the Old and New Testaments because without listening there can be no covenant.

Just as we learn about deep or compassionate listening through the way in which our relationship with the holy rests on our listening to divine text or the will of the universe, so can we learn in the way that the divine listens deeply and compassionately to us.[41] The Breslov Chassidic Jews have a practice developed by their rabbi, Rebbe Nachman, called *hitbodedut*, literally "self-seclusion." Basically, for an hour every day the devout spend time, ideally outside in nature, pouring their heart out to God, as they would, in Rebbe Nachman's words, "to a true, good friend."[42] Rabbi Ozer Bergman[43] describes the process in detail and explains how, when one is being listened to with the depth and compassion of the divine, one naturally moves deeper and deeper both to the true sources of the issues and to a closer connection with the spirit of the divine. Not surprisingly, the path one takes in *hitbodedut* follows a parallel path through the inner depths of the four worlds, which Bergman describes as increasingly inner chambers from the "refuge/recovery room" to the "conference room" to the "bedroom" and finally to the "no-place."

Sufi practice moves similarly through the four worlds, and the third, *marifah*, the world of perception or intuition, is discerned through "the eye of the heart," by which the underlying holiness of the universe becomes increasingly apparent.[44]

Learning to Listen from the Heart

"You ain't learnin' nothin' when you're talkin'!"
—Sid Richardson, Texas oilman, rancher,
and philanthropist (1891–1959)

So to truly hear the source of anger or frustration in another and find a common point of entry for dialogue, we need to learn to listen at a whole different level, from the heart. Coming from the West, where it seems that the more one speaks, the more authority one has, this is a difficult concept to, well, *grok*. And harder still to put into practice.

If people in the West think seriously about listening at all, they usually refer to "active listening," a common set of skills taught regularly in communication and conflict workshops: Pay attention to your body language, elicit information through questioning, repeat main points, use "I" not "you" statements, and talk about the future, not the past. The main points of "active listening" are listed here, with more detail in box 6.8:

- *Repeat main points.* Repeat the main points of the speaker (this lets the speaker know that they have really been heard, a powerful psychological message, and helps focus the dialogue).

- *Ask.* Ask (nonthreatening) questions. Useful both to better understand the speaker and to reassure them that you are really listening.

- *"I" not "you" statements.* When speaking, speak in the first person —"I," not "you"—setting a tone that is more reflective and less confrontational.

compare w/ next page + p. 121

BOX 6.8

ACTIVE LISTENING

Paying Attention
- Face the person who is talking.
- Notice the speaker's body language; does it match what he or she is saying?
- Listen in a place that is free of distractions, so that you can give undivided attention.
- Don't do anything else while you are listening.

Eliciting
- Make use of "encouragers" such as "Can you say more about that?" or "Really?"
- Use a tone of voice that conveys interest.
- Ask open questions to elicit more information.
- Avoid overwhelming the speaker with too many questions.
- Give the speaker a chance to say what needs to be said.
- Avoid giving advice or describing when something similar happened to you.

Reflecting
- Occasionally paraphrase the speaker's main ideas, if appropriate.
- Occasionally reflect the speaker's feelings, if appropriate.
- Check to make sure your understanding is accurate by saying, "It sounds like what you mean is _____. Is that so?" or "Are you saying that you're feeling _____?"

Source: Edy Kaufman, "Innovative Problem-Solving Workshops," in Second Track/Citizens' Diplomacy: Concepts and Techniques for Conflict Transformation, *ed. John Davies and Edy Kaufman (Lanham, MD: Rowman & Littlefield, 2002), 220.*

Figure 6.9. Bench conversation (by Michael Coghlan [CC BY-SA 2.0, desaturated from the original], via https://www.flickr.com/photos/mikecogh/).

- *Future, not history.* Speak in the future or present tense, not the past. This further reduces the possibility of accusations and allows greater cooperation to build a common future.

These are terrific skills for almost all interpersonal disputes and business interactions, and they should definitely be practiced and mastered by all. Stephen Covey's popular *The 7 Habits of Highly Effective People* has an entire chapter on listening deeply, which he calls "empathetic communication."[45] The title of the chapter alludes to an important principle of deep listening: "Seek first to understand, then to be understood."

Covey, reportedly a devout Mormon, may or may not have been aware of the "Prayer of St. Francis,"[46] the second section of which is as follows:

O divine Master, grant that I may not so much seek
To be consoled as to console,
To be understood as to understand,
To be loved as to love.

For it is in giving that we receive;

It is in pardoning that we are pardoned;

It is in dying to self that we are born to eternal life.

This is a critical lesson, reassuring to those who are concerned that by focusing on listening we are giving up on the things that are important for us in favor of the issues of the other. (utilitarian)

BOX 6.9

THE SACRED ART OF LISTENING, FROM THE LISTENING CENTER

One of the keys to developing the capacity to listen more deeply is daily practice. Most of us know that if we want to excel at any skill we need to practice. It is in the daily practice, the spiritual discipline, that we prepare ourselves to listen. Then, when we need to listen deeply, we will be able to focus on the speaker, remaining fully present and aware of what they are saying and who they are being. Becoming a listening presence is critical to learning how to understand the other.

Cultivating Silence: There is no listening without silence. Listening to the silence, listening beyond words is also called contemplative listening. It's about taking time to be quiet and simply be. Getting comfortable with silence is a practice that will transform your capacity to listen.

Slowing Down to Reflect: Reflective listening is listening to yourself—your True Self—getting to know the voice of your soul. Once we learn to know and trust this voice, we find ourselves able to recognize when we need to speak and when we need to listen.

Becoming Present: Deep listening occurs at the heart level. It is present when we feel most connected to another person or to a group of people. Our hearts expand and our capacity to communicate with those of differing beliefs and customs increases.

Three Daily Practices: 1. Silence: Spend at least a minute each day in silence. Use intention to listen for God, source, wisdom. 2. Reflection: Take a deep breath before you respond, listen to your soul—get to know yourself. 3. Presence: Be mindful of each moment, pay attention—be with the person you are with.

"Being listened to is so close to being loved that most people cannot tell the difference."

—David Augsburger, Mennonite theologian, Fuller Theological Seminary

Source: All material © Kay Lindahl, The Sacred Art of Listening (Woodstock, VT: Skylight Paths Publishing, 2002), available online at http://www.sacredlistening.com/tlc_listening101.htm. Used with permission.

This is profoundly untrue. Deciding to listen first is "simply" a question of strategy, where we decide what kind of conversation to have. We could have a conversation at a place of positions and anger, which actually is a natural response when agitation and anger come our way. But think about it: Have you ever been persuaded about something important by someone who was screaming at you? Or accusing you of something? Not likely. Having a positional discussion only scratches the surface of the issue, and anger meeting anger means that little actual communication is going on.

To communicate at a more productive level, we choose to listen first. As we listen, *truly* listen, the anger of the other is likely to dissipate, and the vulnerability underlying the anger and the values underlying the positions and interests will eventually emerge. Moreover, once the other person has had the opportunity to vent, and they feel that you have made an unequivocal attempt to understand them, more often than not they will be willing to listen to you.

~

For 5 years, I worked with the U.S. Bureau of Reclamation, the agency responsible for managing most federal water projects in the seventeen western U.S. states. Increasingly, as values change and most of the biggest projects have already been built, their central task has evolved from technical and construction based to management and process based. Often, agents are in a room with representatives across both political and management spectrums trying to figure out how to meet as many needs as possible. Not surprisingly, their agents often encounter more than their fair share of anger.

One of our joint projects involved developing conflict management coursework specific to the needs of the agency. In such courses, I usually spend at least a half day, if not a full day, simply on the art of listening.

A few months after I gave a course in a bureau office, I got a call from one of the agents.

"It actually works!" she said, sounding a bit surprised.

"How do you mean?" I asked.

She explained that they had spent years in dialogue with a group of stakeholders around a small dam that the bureau owned and managed; the dam had outlived its usefulness and the bureau wanted to remove it. One of the landowners on the reservoir's edge was irate at every stakeholder meeting and would often call the bureau office and just yell at whomever answered, often for minutes on end. In fact, employees had developed a rotation of sorts in the office so that no one got stuck being on the receiving end of the landowner's ire too often.

Well after the agent had taken the course, she decided to test out her skills by calling the landowner on her own. She ended up listening to him for more than 3 hours, and she likened the process of letting his anger dissipate until his vulnerability came through to "letting the spool unthread all the way." For 3 hours the conversation was about the bureau and all the ways they were horrible managers of the public's resources, but somewhere in the last 9 minutes the conversation shifted organically to why he was so upset: a technical issue having to do with silt and his dock. Once they got there, the agent and landowner were able to discuss a strategy for addressing the problem, and he felt comfortable that she understood him completely and that she would advocate for him within the process.

The agent's public affairs officer had been surprised that the agent had wanted to talk to the landowner but had given permission. After the exchange, the supervisor sent around a note of commendation for the agent, including this:

> As she [the agent] explained to me, it was really important to him to be heard. [The agent's] calling him is an example of exceptional customer service, since, based on [the landowner's] letters, he was pretty upset, and she was likely opening herself up to some verbal abuse. But, as it turned out, he was quite pleased that she called him, and they had a very positive and productive conversation.
>
> As the agent said to me, "He [the landowner] told me I was the first person in the agency who ever listened to him."

So deciding to listen is vital, and active listening is a profoundly useful skill for most settings. If there is real pain or deep emotion present in the discussion, however, we need to move to another realm of listening. Active listening calls for speaking in "future, not past." Avoiding the past for people who have experienced either individual or collective trauma sim-ply avoids any chance of recognition, legitimacy, and, ultimately, healing. Moreover, eliciting information is terrific in polite conversation, but when real energy is present, it has the disadvantage of introducing the listener, with all their baggage and agendas, when often what's needed is simply to be present for the speaker. Advice is often much less useful than simple compassionate presence.

Although active listening is a way to facilitate many discussions, when real energy is present we put more emphasis on compassionate, deep, or transformative listening. It is such a powerful and crucial skill that I would argue it is actually the heart of conflict transformation.

Figure 6.10. "Go" game board (© 2017 Caryn M. Davis. Used with permission).

BOX 6.11

TRANSFORMATIVE, COMPASSIONATE, DEEP LISTENING

Context: When real emotion is present, classic problem-solving approaches to dialogue are generally not practical, and "active" listening is too, well, active.

When someone with whom you are in dialogue is clearly distraught, and "objective" problem-solving seems not to be viable, it may be worth stepping back for a few moments, giving the participant the space and time to work through the issue. In such a setting, a listener should take over (often the mediator or facilitator) in a process of "transformative listening." Here, in contrast to "active listening," the listener is not trying to facilitate a healthy dialogue but rather is making himself or herself absolutely present for the speaker to get deeply into the issues to find the roots.

When real energy is present, it is *not* helpful to offer

- advice
- reassurance
- opinion
- curiosity
- self-story (how you experienced something similar)
- any other active presence

Instead, be present entirely for the speaker, knowing that resolution comes from within.

- Listen with an open heart.
- Pause often, giving the gift of silence.
- Track or reflect (statements or open-ended clauses).
- Only when speaker's energy allows (stop if grief or mourning; just be present):
  - Ask permission.
  - Offer without insistence.
  - Check for completeness.

Source: Uzi Weingarten, "Communicating with Compassion," course now offered at http://uzi teaches.com/. Used with permission.

Like many skills requiring presence, they are easy to describe and excruciatingly difficult to master. "Go" is an ancient Chinese game with profoundly simple rules yet deeply nuanced and complex strategy, about which it is said, "A few moments to learn, a lifetime to master."

Just as meditation is "just" paying attention to some focus, such as the breath, transformative listening is "just" being present: offering space

BOX 6.12

FURTHER READING

There are some wonderful sources to learn these deep listening skills. Here are some excellent works on the topic; just let the power of the concepts alluded to in the titles roll off your tongue:

- Kay Lindahl, *The Sacred Art of Listening* (Woodstock, VT: Skylight Paths Publishing, 2002). Available online at http://www.sacredlistening.com /tlc_listening101.htm.
- Andrea S. Cohen, Leah Green, and Susan Partnow, *Practicing the Art of Compassionate Listening* (Indianola, WA: The Compassionate Listening Project, 2011).
- Michael P. Nichols, *The Lost Art of Listening: How Learning to Listen Can Improve Relationships* (New York: The Guilford Press, 1995).
- Mark Brady, ed., *The Wisdom of Listening* (Somerville, MA: Wisdom Publications, 2003).
- Rebecca Z. Shafir, *The Zen of Listening: Mindful Communication in the Age of Distraction* (Wheaton, IL: Quest Books, 2000).
- Mark Nepo, *Seven Thousand Ways to Listen* (New York: Atria Paperback, 2012).

There are also a couple of nice videos online, including a TEDx talk on the subject by Leon Berg, who draws on the native custom of council and listening circles in "The Power of Listening: An Ancient Practice for Our Future: Leon Berg at TEDxRedondoBeach," https://www.youtube.com/watch?v=6i DMuB6NjNA&feature=youtu.be.

Gregorio Billikopf Encina at the University of California, Berkeley, makes available a mediation book and a fifteen-part Listening Skills seminar, "Listening First Aid": http://nature.berkeley.edu/ucce50/ag-labor/7article/article40.htm.

Besides reading about the skills, it is useful to do the kind of coursework that allows practice in a safe setting.

- Marshall Rosenberg's Nonviolent Communications workshops are offered by certified instructors worldwide (Rosenberg died in 2015): https://www.cnvc.org/trainingcal.
- Same with the Compassionate Listening Project, founded by Leah Green (Cohen, Green, and Partnow, http://www.compassionatelistening.org, as noted above), which is a concise and practical workbook that helps one learn many of the skills alluded to in this chapter. Their wonderful workbook offers both a framework and exercises to help learn to listen distinctly for facts, feelings, and values. They offer a "trigger recognition worksheet" and a "self-calming" worksheet, based on the four worlds, to help identify our own triggers and strategize how to transform the energy effectively.
- One of the best courses I have ever taken was "Communicating with Compassion," taught in person and distance-ed by Uzi Weingarten: http://uzi teaches.com.

and silence, or tracking statements, as appropriate and without insisting, checking for completeness, and most crucially allowing the speaker to do the internal work necessary to get at their *own* root causes of discord and to start to work out their *own* path to healing.

These are skills that can be taught, and one finds models in most cultures. Many who have spoken to a thoughtful Buddhist monk report that during the conversation they feel that they are the center of the universe. In *Mindful Mediation*, John McConnell describes listening from a Buddhist perspective:

> We must listen in such a way that we establish *kusala-mūla* (wholesome roots of action) . . . in such a way that we are aware of the processes of meaning-building taking place in our own minds.[47]

Prof. Father José Galván, who teaches at the Department of Moral Theology at the Pontificia Università della Santa Croce in Rome, and who is a parish priest in his "spare time," describes the meditative state he enters when listening to confession, reporting that he feels simply like a conduit, that he is not actually himself a separate entity.[48]

That sense of disappearing into a common source is widespread when deeply listening or, for that matter, when being deeply listened to. Rebbe Nachman of Breslov, the Chassidic leader who urged his followers to the practice of *hitbodedut*, describes how, in intent prayer, the rest of the parishioners dissipate around him, until it's just him and God. "And then," he says, "it's just God."

Transmitting from the Heart

Listening from the heart opens a connection, and as science is slowly catching up to faith traditions in learning, the connection is more profound and elementary than previously thought.

In chapter 4 we discussed the underlying interconnectedness of the universe as a whole, a concept common to most faith traditions; just as Einstein's great contribution to physics is that the entire universe is either energy or potential energy, a more spiritual understanding would be that all existence is either life energy (or consciousness) or potential life energy (or consciousness).

Table 6.3
Energy/Life Force around the World

Greek	Pneuma
Polynesian	Mana
Hebrew	Ruah
Sanskrit	Prana
Chinese	Chi
Japanese	Ki
Ancient Egyptian	Ka
German	Lebenskraft
Tibetan	Lung
Persian	Rooh

This underlying matter–energy–life force is described worldwide and throughout the ages (table 6.3).[49]

Religious thinkers describe our interaction with this life force through, for instance, prayer, meditation, or nature. In his famous *Autobiography of a Yogi*, Paramhansa Yogananda explains,

> The different sensory stimuli to which man reacts—tactual, visual, gustatory, auditory, and olfactory—are produced by vibratory variations in electrons and protons. The vibrations in turn are regulated by "lifetrons," subtle life forces or finer-than-atomic energies intelligently charged with the five distinctive sensory idea-substances.[50]

In this sense, when we connect with each other it is through this medium, allowing both fundamental connection and access to deep truths, what we call intuition.

Science, thankfully, is catching up. Psychology has long known that emotions are contagious, but we are finding not only the physical medium but also that the heart is actually a powerful, measurable transmitter. In Daniel Goleman's podcast on leadership and emotional intelligence, he focuses on the brain and our mood's "contagiousness" through mirror neurons, which fire in relationship to someone else. Among peers it seems that the most powerful emotion leads, but in organizations, the leader's mood projects onto the others. If a leader is in a positive mood, so will the group be, creating a powerful incentive to lead through positivity. More-

Figure 6.11. *Practicing Sahaja Yoga in a park in Israel, 2015 (by Marie Sahaj [Own work] [CC BY-SA 4.0, desaturated from original], via Wikimedia Commons from Wikimedia Commons).*

over, as emotions transmit from one to another, even heart rates align, in what he calls "the physiology of entrainment."[51]

Similar but surprisingly separate research is confirming that the heart is also a carrier and transmitter of energy and emotion. Some suggest that the heart has its own nervous system, enabling it to learn, remember, and make functional decisions independent of the brain's cerebral cortex. The heart is in regular neurotransmitting communication with the brain, actually sending more information to the brain than the other way around, and it generates an electromagnetic field that extends several feet outside the body.

In short, taking the two strands of scientific inquiry together, we are finally learning to understand religious allusions to the "listening heart," the "thinking heart," and the "heart-mind." We seem to be edging toward scientific confirmation of the power and truth of intuition and of being "tapped in" to the people and forces around us.

What does any of this mean to us as we work through our interpersonal differences?

It turns out that we can use our "energy field" consciously, actually measurably calming someone who is agitated simply by being present with them in a calming way. This is no surprise to many: Calming someone else through shared presence is a common Buddhist technique, one that I learned from Phra Paisan Visalo, a Buddhist monk of the Thai Forest tradition. Part of the practice is to match the rate of breathing of the other person, then gently to slow one's own rate down, which in turn slows their rate as well, all without their knowledge.

> Silence also teaches us how to speak. . . . Before we speak, whether to share our own experience or to reflect on another's, we listen in the silence. From this *makom*, this grounding in silence, we enter the *Makom*, the presence of God. This is the stance of Elijah at the cave, finding God in the "still, small voice"[52]—literally, "the thin voice of silence." From that place of deeper listening, not to each other but to God, the Holy, the deeper inner wisdom of our souls, we find the words that encourage each other to claim the truth and mystery of our lives.

What "trains" us to be spiritual companions for each other? The silence.[53]

In the same podcast series mentioned above, George Kohlrieser describes his use of presence and mirroring in his practice as a mediator.[54] Erica Ariel Fox, initiator of the Harvard Negotiation Insight Initiative, writes of tapping into intuition in conflictive settings. She suggests that whereas Western mediators are trained to "engage their minds . . . and think through the next move," more experienced mediators, what she calls master practitioners, "relax their minds, listen into the force field, and perceive what is needed." She uses the language of *Star Wars* to elaborate:[55]

> We suggest it is a skill, not magic, that these expert practitioners employ when they make instinctive judgment calls. In negotiating conflict, we believe that learning to read, follow and use the real-life "force" is the highest leverage intervention one can make. More importantly, we suggest that tuning into the interpenetrating force field around us is something one can teach and learn.

Walking the Path Together: Other Practical Tools for Addressing the Conflict between Us

As I've said, listening from the heart is connecting. But then what? We've seen, from a practical level, that connecting at this level can help alleviate anger and other blocks to effective communication while allowing careful identification of shared values that in turn become entry ways for dialogue.

Besides the skills of deep listening and reframing for values, many teachers and traditions offer practical tools that can be helpful at this interpersonal scale:

- Walk the Four Parallels. Gershon Winkler describes using what he calls the Four Parallels of "the shamanic in Judaism"—literal, allegorical, interpretive, and mystery—to guide through and past frustration in "the Sacred Walk." He gives an example of being triggered by something his child may be doing that, if he remains in the literal place, could result in anger and frustration. Rather, he slips through the Parallels to ask what he is being shown at that moment, resulting in easing and calming of his emotions, "surrendering to the mystery place," where his work and commitments ease away, and finally moving to the sacred solitude in the Great Void, "where nothing exists other than the Great Mystery we call 'God,' manifested in my selfhood and in the selfhood of my child."[56]

- Pause for the "golden quarter second." When one is triggered, it can be very difficult to move into a place where listening can be productive. In trainings on the "Chemistry of Connection," psychologists Daniel Goleman and Tara Bennett-Goleman talk about the "golden quarter second," the time between an "amygdala capture," where one's flight-or-fight instincts take over the brain in response to an apparent physical, emotional, perceptual, or spiritual threat, and a state of conscious awareness of the situation. The golden quarter second, though, is the next gap, the time between awareness and the capacity to act. The moment one has a sense of being triggered, it is crucial to give oneself the time to craft a productive response. Here, I recommend going back to the last chapter's three steps: stop, breathe, and listen. Giving oneself the time to understand both one's own vulnerability and why it may have been triggered, as well as the motivations of the other, allows both parties to meet in a place of mutual interests and shared values.

- Look for the spark of the divine. One tool from spiritual traditions around the world, and one that can be drawn upon in the golden quarter second, is to learn to look for the "spark of the divine" in the other. Regardless of who they are or how they may be contributing to your triggers, those with spiritual training often shift their perspective to reflect that the protagonist is God's creation, crafted with holy light, in Hebrew *tzelem Elohim*. This is a powerful reminder to look for the good, the vulnerable, or the holy in every interaction. Al-Hallaj, the Sufi poet, writes, "I saw my Lord with the eye of the Heart. I said: 'Who are you?' He answered: 'You.'"[57]

- The creative use of silence can be extraordinarily powerful. Either simply pausing to allow for silence or explicitly asking for a moment of reflection may help untangle a difficult setting: "Silence your lips from speaking, your heart from thinking, and if your mouth is running to speak, and your heart is racing to think, return to the Place."[58] Similarly, *kriya* yoga is a technique whereby "the sensory tumult is stilled, permitting man to achieve an ever-increasing identity with cosmic consciousness."[59]

- On a lighter note, Sufi master Fara Gaye advocates the judicious use of laughter as a way to connect.[60]

- Use divine attributes to evaluate agreements. An interesting intellectual exercise, posed by Dr. Shaiya Rothberg of the Conservative Yeshiva in Jerusalem, a Kabbalah scholar, suggests using the thirteen divine attributes seen in box 6.1 to evaluate agreements between individuals for their ethics and equity. One might use similar sets of attributes from other traditions, such as the *Paramitas* (transcendental actions) listed on the same page, because each offers the potential to elevate the conversation and authority beyond most common scales in use today.

- Michelle LeBaron describes conflicts as having three levels (which mirror our first three worlds): those that are material, often disputes over scarce resources; relational, between individuals; and symbolic. For the material, she advocates analysis and problem solving; for relational, she suggests active listening, restating, and reframing; and for the symbolic, she advocates the use of metaphor, ritual, and narrative. As described in this chapter, she suggests starting at the highest level, then working "backwards." She offers that ritual is about a shift: One can notice when shifts happen, often through informal ritual. She suggests naming it and asking, "Did we notice what happened? How can we build on that?"[61]

- Marshall Rosenberg, whose workshops and books on nonviolent communications I referenced earlier, has a remarkably effective approach to dialogue, in which he advocates a simple process of (naturally) four steps: Observe the situation accurately, notice one's feelings associated with the situation, identify the needs that are not being met, and make a request for whatever is needed of the other.[62]

~

To sum, why is listening at the heart of conflict transformation? I suggest three reasons:

- The process of understanding interests and values behind positions is key to moving dialogue forward, and the best way to discover one's interests and values is to listen deeply to where one might feel these are being threatened.

- Anger and frustration are generally shields protecting vulnerability. One can have a conversation filled with anger and frustration, or alternatively, one might allow the space through transformative listening for the anger to dissipate and have a healthier conversation addressing the underlying vulnerability.

- People will generally listen once they themselves have been listened to.

By using values as an entryway and transformative listening as a central approach, I want to be clear that I am not suggesting that positions and interests do not need to be addressed, nor that anger is something to be avoided. Having the space to vent about perceived or actual past wrongs is often a key to moving a dialogue forward productively. Swami Subodhananda of the Chinmaya Ashram in Sidhbari, India, suggests a Hindu perspective that, as we have mentioned, the source of anger is internal, built from desire. When one decides that bliss comes from outside, it leads to unhealthy passion and other destructive emotions. And yet anger is natural—"Heat can't leave the fire," he says, "it's part of its nature"—and can have positive aspects. It can protect one from harm or be an instrument of discipline, for example. Nonetheless, learning to harness it or al-

---

BOX 6.13

TAKE-HOME MESSAGE

When anger, whether in you or in others, signals vulnerability:

1. Stop
2. Breathe
3. Listen

Figure 6.12. *Packing relief kits for tsunami victims (by Lou Anderson/AusAID [CC BY 2.0, desaturated from the original], via https://www.flickr.com/photos /dfataustralianaid/).*

low it to manifest in a productive way requires "a lot of *sadhana*—spiritual practice." The best use of the power that it brings, he advises, is to help others.[63]

To illustrate, let's go back to the balcony in the Mekong Basin where I took a break with one of the delegates who simply said "no" to everything that was proposed in the meeting on transboundary environmental impacts. Recall from the beginning of the chapter that she was in the middle of venting about the other delegates, how they were bullies trying to take advantage of her generosity. Despite the relative calm of the balcony and lush garden that it overlooked, as well as our one-on-one setting, she was able to keep her ire up for close to 10 minutes, with just about every sentence starting with the word "they" or "them."

As I did my best to listen in empathy, from my heart, I could see that there was real pain underneath her anger, real vulnerability, but I could not quite intuit the source. That's one of the key points of this kind of listening: In order to get deeper into the issue, the speaker is the one who finally does the work.

Sure enough, as the anger started to dissipate and she started to run out of "they" sentences, she would let slip an occasional comment on her own team and her concern that they too were being taken advantage of.

Every time she paused, all I would do is try to give her space to continue to work through the issue. When people pause in dialogue, they often will give important cues as to what they are looking for. If they look up or down, they are still working inside, and my approach is simply to continue to be present in silence. Inevitably they will keep going after a moment, often one level deeper. If they look at me rather than looking up or down, they usually want a simple word of reassurance that I am still there with them, in which case a useful skill is tracking, simply repeating the last important thing I heard, not as a question but simply as a statement. That reassures them that I am there, present, and hearing them. Again, more often than not, they will continue on.

Finally, though, when someone really has gotten to the core of the issue or figured out a direction or solution on his or her own, they will often signal that moment with a tangible sigh of release or relief. It is only at that moment that, after asking permission, I might offer my observations.[64]

Just as she was hitting that moment, she had shifted her comments from "them" to increasingly talk about her worries about her team. And not just that they were being bullied but, finally, she shared her concern about her team's technical capacity to keep up with the professionals in the other countries.

And then she sighed.

So then the vulnerability was clear: She was worried not only about her team's technical capacity but, and probably more importantly in that part of the world, that she, her team, and her country could lose face if their relative lack of skills became apparent.

And then it was clear what our strategy was to move forward. We together went back into the room, and she invited all the other teams to a skill-building workshop in her country that her team would host, inviting trainers from all four countries.

"Because we have all learned these skills in a different manner separately in our own countries," she offered, "it would be helpful for us all to learn a unified way—a Mekong way—of getting on the same page and doing the work together."

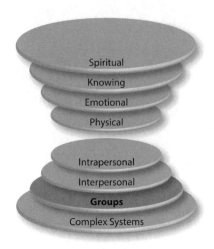

Figure 7.1.

Table 7.1
Needs, Expressions, and Stages of Dialogue

Four Worlds and Foundational Needs	Four Expressions: Pursuit of Needs in Dialogue and Negotiations	ARIA: Four Stages of Group Dialogue
Physical	Positions	Adversarial
Emotional	Interests	Reflective
Perceptual	Values	Integrative
Spiritual	Harmony	Action

Figure 7.2. *Bharata places Rama's sandals on the throne. (Original painting by Kate Hirons, from "The Ramayana, in a Nutshell" [http://imagination-chariot. blogspot.com/], used with permission.*

CHAPTER SEVEN

Rama's Sandals and Other Lessons for Groups

Mbunto—Humanity: a person is a person because of other people. —Zulu saying

The Ramayana describes Rama's exile at his stepmother's behest, so that her son Bharata would become king instead. Bharata, distraught, goes to Rama's forest retreat and begs Rama to return and rule, but Rama refuses to disobey the decree. Bharata then takes Rama's sandals saying, "I will put these on the throne, and every day I shall place the fruits of my work at the feet of my Lord." Embracing Rama, he takes the sandals and returns to Aydohya.

In modern-day India, Hindu deities are actually the legal owners of temples dedicated to them. As such, they become official stakeholders in issues relating to the temple or surrounding lands or water. Often, in stakeholder meetings, their presence is represented by a pair of sandals on a chair, in allusion to Bharata's example. Participants report that the sense of having a deity in the room has a definite impact in the tenor of discussion.

"Bureau, Reclaim Thyself!"

As I mentioned in chapter 6, I worked with the U.S. Bureau of Reclamation, the agency responsible for managing most federal water projects in the seventeen western U.S. states, for the better part of 5 years to help bolster the agency's capacity in conflict management and transformation.

This involved research into actual causes of conflict in the U.S. West (*not* necessarily water scarcity, as had been commonly assumed, but mostly how new laws and regulations were implemented), and into the reward system of the agency itself (managers who resolved conflicts after they had blown up rose faster and earned more than those who managed conflicts from the early stages or prevented them entirely). We also collaborated on a series of skills-building courses and facilitated stakeholder meetings, activities that can be combined for better effect. If a dialogue is couched in the educational setting of a course—say, as an exercise or as the focus of skills-building exercises—the pressure of formal negotiations is often relieved to some extent, and hot-button issues can be discussed while developing the skills for discussing such issues.

So that's what I was doing in yet another nondescript meeting room of a national chain hotel in a southwestern state, with a room of about twenty representatives from different sides of an issue related to an endangered species and an irrigation project, about a third of whom were bureau employees.

Dialogue was fairly cordial, especially with most of the nonfederal representatives, many of whom had been meeting for years. Although these representatives were nominally on very different sides of the issues, they saw that they could make progress only together, and, furthermore, they had developed warm personal relations over their countless meetings. Even so, I kept picking up on subtle barbs between a couple of individuals in the room, which seemed odd because those individuals all worked for the same agency, the Bureau of Reclamation.

The digs didn't seem personal but rather referenced different approaches to natural resource management, often in code: One side was accused of being "cowboys running roughshod," whereas the others "appeared to like fish more than people."

Because the bureau was the host agency, it would have been difficult to proceed while exhibiting such internal discord, so again it was time for the "balcony." Most participants took the afternoon for a hastily organized field trip, while the bureau folks stayed back for "internal capacity building." Together, we worked with a toolbox of techniques to facilitate small group dialogue.

In this chapter, we will focus on the group scale, moving through the four worlds as our guide. My assumption is that many reading this book will either be responsible for designing and leading such discussions or regularly participate in them. Most of our world seems to be run on meetings, and one can help the process either through a formal leadership role or simply by being a more effective participant. Either way, the material on which to draw is extensive and is rarely explicitly tapped in conflict training in the West (with a few notable exceptions, described in chapter 2). But both Bahá'í and Quaker writings have explicit descriptions for facilitating difficult discussions, and most traditions have developed clear tools for creating settings that offer greater potential for mutual understanding, respect, and even transformation.

In the previous chapter, we described how centering on values is a useful entryway for dialogue with another, focusing on core issues that we have in common, even as we back into the critical issues of interests and positions that brought us into the room to begin with. We also spent a lot of time with the concept of listening from the heart as a way to identify the values one is seeking to protect.

Working in groups is little different, except that the process becomes exponentially more complicated as more and more people are involved. Nonetheless, we still look for shared values, balancing the needs of self and other is still paramount, and deep listening is still a profound approach to help us through.

Some specialists at the World Bank, for example, when they are working with stakeholders on major development projects, will use group values as performance criteria, that is, the metrics by which success will be measured, such as "alleviating poverty" or "protecting the environment." Once values are embedded in the process, the specialists circle back as the project is designed, then implemented, and check that the values as expressed by the group have been upheld.[1] Susan O'Malley Wade, a manager of strategic and sustainability planning at the San Francisco Public Utilities Commission, has written a helpful article on "Using Intentional, Values-Based Dialogue to Engage Complex Public Policy Conflicts," in which she writes,

Values are the key. Intentional, values-based dialogue relies on bringing to the fore and engaging the values underlying different experiences, views, and interests. This reliance is premised on the notion that the conflict resulting from these value differences is natural to the creative human impulse to explore meaning and to improve conditions.[2]

An example: A recent dialogue in the western United States about trying to increase minimum flows in a stream nominally pitted environmentalists against farmers against tribes. After several unsuccessful meetings that dissolved into discord, it was decided to go out and visit a site that each side thought was important. As each representative presented their views—one at a fish hatchery, one by an irrigated field, and one at the reservation longhouse—the role of the others was simply to listen. As each spoke and was assured the space to continue without being challenged, the initial positions ("We need the water on the farms." "The fish will die unless it's put back in the stream.") gave way to the core values underlying the discussion: the deep love each had for the land and the water, and the larger threats to livelihoods, shared ecosystems, and ways of life. Although positions did not change, the conversation going forward was able to tap into those shared values and address them explicitly in a way that eventually made a shared strategy possible. Leading with values, understood through listening, becomes the core of fruitful dialogue regardless of how many people are involved.

And, as ever, the four worlds offer guidance.

An example from the Middle East reminds us that even our words can be understood differently depending on the lens through which we view them. The mediator or facilitator can harness the construct and sequence of the four worlds to facilitate new understanding. In contrast, we ignore the four worlds at our peril.

As peace negotiations between Israelis and Arabs commenced in the early 1990s, for example, each side approached their construct of "water" very differently. From the Palestinian and Jordanian side, the concept of "water" was conceptualized in a very physical sense (people literally did not have enough clean water in some cases for sustenance) or in an

Figure 7.3. Coquille Indian Tribal members paddle a canoe in the Ni-les'tun Marsh for the first time in more than 140 years. The reclamation and re-creation of a tidal marsh at Bandon Marsh National Wildlife Refuge was a large, complex collaborative project involving federal, state, tribal, and private partners and landowners (photo by Roy W. Lowe/USFWS [CC BY-NC 2.0; used with permission]).

emotional sense (control over water as representing larger issues of sovereignty and occupation). From the Israeli side, "water" was constructed intellectually: Survival had long been assured, so the challenge was to move, price, treat, and store water in the most efficient manner.

These conflicting conceptualizations led to both difficult impasses—water was the last issue concluded in the Israel–Jordan Treaty of Peace—but also to especially creative solutions. In what will no doubt become a classic modification of the tenets of international law, Israelis and Jordanians invented legal terminology to suit particularly local requirements in their 1994 peace treaty. In negotiations leading up to the treaty, Israelis, making the intellectual argument that the entire region was running out of water, insisted on discussing only water "allocations," that is, the future needs of each riparian. Jordanians, in contrast, refused to discuss the future until past grievances had been addressed; they would not negotiate "allocations" until the historic physical and emotional question of water "rights" had been resolved.

There is little room to bargain between the past and the future, between "rights" and "allocations." Negotiations reached an impasse until one of the mediators suggested the term "rightful allocations" to describe simultaneously historic claims and future goals for cooperative projects. This new term is now immortalized in the water-related clauses of the Israel–Jordan Treaty of Peace.

As for the fourth world, we can see that, globally, native and indigenous peoples see "water" as a holistic, spiritual resource. With the construct of the four worlds, we can conceptualize how jarring, to the point of sacrilegious, it can be to approach problem solving in "rational," economic concepts as, for example, when the suggestion is made to use water from a Hopi sacred spring to transport coal slurry across the state of New Mexico.

The Four Worlds and Their Expression in Groups

As with intrapersonal and interpersonal disputes, there are no blueprints for group dynamics where competing interests are being expressed. However, one might think of an idealized process that builds on patterns that have been observed over time. "Classic" water disputes between, for example, developers and environmentalists, rural and urban users, or upstream and downstream riparians suggest zero-sum confrontations where one party's loss is another's gain and where confrontation seems inevitable. Yet such "intractable" differences are regularly and commonly addressed as creative thinking and human ingenuity allow solutions that draw on a more intricate understanding of both water and conflict to come to the fore.

This section offers one path to the transformation of group disputes from zero-sum, intractable differences to positive-sum, creative solutions, and centers on a migration of thought generally through, not surprisingly, our four worlds. For group dynamics, we look at how the worlds are expressed collectively in an idealized process and build on the work and experience of Jay Rothman and his ARIA[3] model of stages of dialogue: adversarial, reflexive, integrative, and action.[4]

Note that, like the four worlds, all stages exist simultaneously and not necessarily in sequence. Furthermore, there is not necessarily a "right" stage that must be achieved for "success." In today's world, many disputes never move beyond the first or second stage, yet they are tremendously resilient, and a few have achieved the fourth stage and are fraught with tension. Nevertheless, like any skill, it is useful to understand the structure of an "ideal" path, in order to perfect the tools needed for any individual situation.

The generalized path described here is structured around an understanding of each of the four stages through any of four perspectives, as described in table 7.2.

In its initial setting, conflict is perceived as *adversarial* and competitive. Participants are focused on their positions, and thinking is framed in "us versus them." Dialogue is often focused on the past, based on the rights to which one feels entitled, and a period of expressing pent-up grievances and venting can be necessary. Inefficient and inequitable proposals are all but inevitable during this stage of dialogue. As a consequence of these initial tensions, collaborative learning and trust-building exercises are key, notably on active and transformative listening, as described in the previous chapter.

There are skills that can be developed at this level to build greater understanding and more mutually satisfying outcomes. Collaborative learning, for example, allows groups to jointly define a problem, which helps lay groundwork for management and transformation.[5] At this stage, emphasis is on self-awareness of how we communicate and perceive situations and on trust-building. These can open us up to the possibility that there is more to a situation than we originally thought and help us be willing to listen to other perspectives without believing that we need to change them.

As the adversarial stage of dialogue plays out, occasionally some cracks can be seen in the strict, rights-based positions of each side (although at least in actual water negotiations, this process can last decades). Eventually, and sometimes painfully, a shift can start to take place where the parties begin to listen a bit more and where the interests underlying the positions start to become a bit apparent. In this second, *reflexive* stage,

Table 7.2
Needs, Expressions, and Stages of Dialogue

Four Foundational Needs	Four Expressions of Needs in Negotiations	The ARIA of Group Dynamics
Physical	Positions	Adversarial
Emotional	Interests	Reflective
Perceptual	Values	Integrative
Spiritual	Harmony	Action

dialogue can shift from rights (what someone feels they are entitled to) to requirements (what is actually needed to fulfill their goals).

In water negotiations, for example, countries often start by focusing on the water rights they feel they are due, either because more rain originates within their territory or because they have been using the water longer. Think Nile, where 75 to 85 percent of the flow originates in upstream Ethiopia, while downstream Egypt has counted on uninterrupted flow for its use for millennia. Currently, they are modifying their stances to focus on what is actually needed for their planned hydropower and agricultural development.

Conceptually, it is as if we have removed the national boundaries from the map and can for the first time assess the needs of the "watershed" as a whole. This shift, from speaking to listening, from rights to requirements, from a figurative basin with boundaries to one without, is a huge and crucial conceptual shift on the part of the participants. It can be profoundly difficult to accomplish yet absolutely vital to achieve for any movement at all toward any sustainable agreement.

The tone is more open. Listening becomes pivotal to success. The process involves all parties with a stake in an issue: those who are affected by the outcome and those in a position to help implement or block implementation of an outcome (i.e., stakeholders). Attempts are made to shift the nature of negotiations to try to increase the amount of resources and to maximize mutual gain.

Once participants have moved through the first two stages from mostly speaking to mostly listening and from thinking about rights to requirements, the problem-solving capabilities inherent to most groups can begin to foster creative, cooperative solutions. In this *integrative* stage, the needs expressed earlier begin to coalesce together to form group interests: the "why" underlying the desire for the resource. Conceptually, we start to add benefits to the still boundary-less map and, in fact, to think about how to enhance benefits to whatever is on the table.

Participants explore reframing the problem for new possibilities and insights. Together they uncover and form a base of shared meaning that can help coordinate and align collective actions and shared values. The focus is on *consensus-building*, and parties think in terms of a "problemshed" or "benefits-shed," and *benefits*—economically, ecologically, and socially through time.

Finally, although tremendous progress has been made over the first three stages, both in terms of group dynamics and in developing cooperative benefits, the last *action* stage helps with tools to guide the sustainable implementation of the plans that have been developed and to make sure that the benefits are distributed equitably among the parties. The scale at this stage is now regional where, conceptually, we need to put the political boundaries back on the map, reintroducing the political interest in seeing that the "baskets" that have been developed are to the benefit of all.

The focus of the action stage is on capacity building, and analysis is on institutional capacity. Governance structures are usually created or adapted to complement existing institutions and structures. These offer the crucible for ongoing discussions, community building, and progress at a human scale, and they are ideally networked with relevant institutions and agencies to meet resource management, restoration, and sustainability goals.

As with the four worlds, the first three components are internal, in this case to the group, and the last is the external manifestation of the group decision. Maybe it is an action plan that is being put into place or an agreement that constituents now need to be brought into. In groups, this shift from internal to external can be especially difficult, because outside constituents have not gone through the bonding or mutual understanding that the group has. Edy Kaufman is a human rights activist originally from Argentina who now splits his time between Israel and the United States. He has described a detailed 2-week healing workshop for communities in crisis.[6] He generally follows the ARIA model and pays special attention to this last stage, with detailed "Guidelines for Going Home."

~

It is critical not to think of these stages as a linear process, where the further along the participants are the better. Most processes ebb and flow back and forth over time, finding the level that meets a particular set of group needs for a given place and time; there is no "right" set of answers. One might think of these all existing in parallel universes simultaneously, each with its own set of approaches or tools, any of which may be useful at any given time, or conceptually as a helix or set of spheres rather than strictly linear. I break them apart here only for the purposes of explanation.

Wisdom Roots of Group Process

Jay Rothman, whose ARIA model is described above, is a scholar and practitioner now based in Israel who has worked with communities in conflict around the world, including Cyprus, Israel, Northern Ireland, the former Soviet Union, and Sri Lanka. I have admired and used his work for years and met him for the first time in 2005 when I was studying Kabbalah in Jerusalem and he was offering a professional workshop in Haifa. When I mentioned the similarities between the four worlds and ARIA, he was unaware but not surprised; he had been exposed to the concepts most of his life, and he allowed that the ethics on which his work was based would naturally influence the structure of his professional model.

As we earlier noted that the four worlds model has global analogs, it's not surprising that four-part structures for group processes likewise exist worldwide.

Phra Paisan Visalo, a Buddhist monk of the Thai Forest tradition and community mediator whom we first met in chapter 6, describes how he uses the Four Foundations of the Buddha's teachings to structure group processes that he designs—processes that he describes as being "all about broadening perspectives." Making sure that drinking water is available and the room is cool attends to participants' physical needs, for example. To attend to their emotional state, he starts by asking each participant to say something nice about someone else in the room. He tries to act as a personal example of treating each other with respect and equanimity, and he feels that his actions influence the flow of the room. For the perceptual level, he helps participants understand the relationship between their own positions and the needs of the community by asking, "If you get what you are asking for, what will be the impact on the community?" And of course his monk's robes and the simple majesty of the temples in which he holds dialogue guarantee that the spiritual component is infused throughout.[7]

Tomas Andres describes how leading negotiations structured on traditional Filipino values is based on aligning one's *loob* or *kalooban*, the inner self, a singular entity composed of the body, emotion, mind, and soul. Once one is cleansed (*Tapat ang loob*), they can begin to facilitate healing process by energy transference.

Group harmony is the goal, through four stages: (1) *Magtapatan ng Loob*, truthful facts and establishment of objectives and aims; (2) *Magkagaangan ng loob*, establishing friendly relationships, with an atmosphere of trust and confidence; (3) *Makuha ng loob*, getting to each other's inner-self or core being; and (4) *Magkapanatagan ng loob*, concentration and trusting problem solving. The result is *kabutihang loob*, happy, successful, and productive relationships, stable in their own area and flexible in details.[8]

Likewise, a central Bahá'í tenet is the process of "consultation," described by Baha'u'allah, the founder of the faith, as "one of the most fundamental elements of the divine edifice":[9]

> The Great Being saith: The heaven of Divine wisdom is illumined with the two luminaries of consultation and compassion. Take ye counsel together in all matters, inasmuch as consultation is the lamp of guidance which leadeth the way, and is the bestower of understanding.

Bahá'í consultation can be defined as a process for sharing thoughts and feelings through talking things out with others in an atmosphere of love and harmony with commitment to accomplishing some definite, common purpose and has four features:

- Release creative energies from the minds and hearts of those involved.

- Offer new understanding and enlightenment to a subject.

Figure 7.4. Leschan, China: Buddhist monk, contemplating in nature. (Photo by CEphoto, Uwe Aranas [CC-BY-SA-3.0]).

- Share appropriate information, ideas, thoughts, feelings, and impressions.
- Provide an atmosphere fostering love, harmony, and unity.

Seven virtues and seven detriments of Bahá'í consultation are offered in table 7.3. Adhering to the virtues and avoiding the detriments are seen as deep spiritual practices.

Likewise, the Evangelical Christian group Peacemaker Ministries offers training and resources worldwide to apply "the powerful conflict resolution principles God has given to us through Scripture."[10] They focus on both resolution of disputes and reconciliation of relationships, and they follow a similar four-stage process (with modern interpretations and reference to the biblical text on which each is based in parentheses):

1. Glorify God (Go to Higher Ground, 1 Corinthians 10:31). Central is asking, "How can I please and honor God in this situation?"

2. Get the Log out of Your Eye (Get Real about Yourself, Matthew 7:5). Encourages examining one's own role in the dispute and giving a thorough and humble confession.

Table 7.3
Virtues and Detriments of Bahá'í Consultation

The Seven Virtues	The Seven Detriments
Motive: Working for the same thing without hidden motives speeds the process along.	Discord: Power plays, ulterior motives, and contention interfere with getting the best ideas.
Spirit: Enthusiasm, positive outlook, and setting aside personal preferences aid in finding good solutions.	Stubbornness: Stubbornness guarantees discord and wrangling and silences the group genius.
Detachment: Ideas belong to the group; once you present an idea, let it go.	Pride of Authorship: Holding preconceived positions or answers conflicts with finding new solutions.
Attraction: Eagerness to hear the contributions of others brings forth better ideas; willingness to consult in a spirit of gladness unalloyed brings joy to the discussion.	Discounting: Putting others or their ideas down stifles the group genius.
Humility: Modesty aids consultation; arrogance or patronizing undermines it.	Advocacy: Each one should present his or her own views and not those of another.
Patience: Along with grace under stress, patience allows the best answers to develop.	Criticism: In or out of the interaction prevents decisions from proving their worth.
Service: An attitude of service gives priority to the group over the self.	Dominating: Superior and subordinate roles should be set aside and ideas considered on merit; winning is working together.

3. Gently Restore (Gently Engage Others, Galatians 6:1). Respectfully and graciously helping others to see how they have contributed.

4. Go and Be Reconciled (Get Together on Lasting Solutions, Matthew 5:24). Focus on preserving and restoring the relationship through forgiveness.

Facilitating the Process

Helping craft a setting and process conducive to transformation through the processes described above requires all the tools at our disposal. Let's go through each of the four worlds and bring to bear offerings from the faith traditions of the world to help facilitate our processes.

Physical

As noted before, thinking through the physical dimensions of gatherings is critical and must be done beforehand. In the West, unfortunately, most meetings I attend are in stark, utilitarian rooms—with no access to food, natural light, or fresh air—where, in general, we get right to work with no preparation or relationship building at all.

So think instead about the physical spaces that bring you peace. Is it a house of worship? A historic building? A patch of forest? Clearly, negotiating a space that is comforting to all participants is, well, a negotiation. If the group is not homogeneous religiously, a house of worship may be more divisive to some than unifying, although if none of the participants is actively antireligious, holding dialogue in a house of worship can definitely have a moderating effect.

And we can at least give the matter some thought. In *Sacred Space*, the authors of five faiths describe ways their places of worship give comfort. What is striking is that none describe expansive architecture or great majesty. Rather it is the smaller things—the cross on the wall, signifying "an ever-present reminder of a God who is not remote from suffering and from the pain and alienation we all feel."[11] It is the *mihrab* in a mosque, and the *mizrach* in a synagogue, each signifiers of the direction of prayer toward, respectively, Mecca and Jerusalem, and each a reminder that some subset of humanity is at that moment aligning themselves with you and your higher intentions from around the world. In temples of Vedic faiths, it is the symbol of AUM, "the holy sound of God," found perhaps above the shrine.

The Baganda people of Uganda set aside an area they call a *kisaakaate*, or enclosure, a village place enclosed in a perimeter wall that was traditionally managed by the village chief:

Figure 7.5. *Cross at a retreat center, Tahlequah (by Jacob Meyer [CC0] via https://unsplash.com/@jamimagery).*

Each village was required to have a *Kisaakaate* as a physical or symbolic place to promote peaceful coexistence, among other services, through which Baganda maintained their unity and made peace with non-Baganda. Participants included both adults and children from different kinship groups and learned about Baganda culture and history. They received training in leadership and acquired skills necessary to serve their families, groups and the kingdom. Chiefs also conducted mock trials to learn and become more effective as judges.[12]

The point is that each of these calls to our higher selves, and even in our secular, utilitarian world, it is worth thinking through whatever evocative spaces we may have at our disposal. On my campus in Corvallis, Oregon, we have access to some wonderful rooms, many with natural light, substantial oak furniture, and windows that open (and many, many spaces that are the diametric opposite). Find what you can. As I mentioned in chapter 4, one group of stakeholders in California found themselves argu-

Figure 7.6. Detail of (a: top) *the* mihrab, *Great Mosque of Córdoba (by Jbribeiro1, Own work [CC BY-SA 3.0, desaturated from the original], via Wikimedia Commons from Wikimedia Commons), and (b: bottom) the* mizrach, *Córdoba Synagogue, Spain (by Harvey Barrison [CC BY-SA 2.0, desaturated from the original and cropped], via https://www.flickr.com/photos /hbarrison/).*

ing loudly whenever they got together, and they put their heads together to try to find a space that would inhibit their shouting. They nicknamed themselves the Library Group for the space they chose.

Although it is difficult in this age of PowerPoints and i-everything, it may actually be worth going outside for at least part of the discussion. As Morihei Ueshiba, the founder of Aikido, noted, "The divine does not like to be shut up in a building. The divine likes to be out in the open. It is right here in this very body. Each one of us is a miniature universe, a living shrine."[13]

Likewise, the seating arrangement, normally offered with adversaries sitting directly opposite from each other, is probably one of the worst energetic arrangements possible, as anger fuels anger through body language and facial expressions. Yet in prayer, regardless of the tradition, we sit side by side, where we shift opposing energy to energy moving in parallel. In our workshops and negotiations, we often put the people with the most difficulty with each other directly side by side, and really, really close together. Whether energetically or psychologically, it is hard to get angry sideways.

Quakers act as mediators around the world, both within their community and without, treating the process as a spiritual practice, and have developed a Friends Conflict Resolution Program to support the practice. The *Mediator's Handbook*[14] has an entire chapter on seating arrangements, depending on the psychology, culture, and spirit of each particular setting.

Food is huge. I am amazed at the number of meetings I attend where this most basic physical component is missing. Beyond nourishment, however, there is a definite intangible benefit when groups share food. Elias Jabour, a Palestinian practitioner of the *sulha*, a traditional peacemaking process of the Arab world, writes, "The eating of a meal together, from ancient times, carries the strength of covenant and is a sign of reconciliation and the removing of barriers from between the participants."[15]

Movies such as *Babette's Feast* and *Like Water for Chocolate* have popularized the idea that food can be infused with emotion—positive emotion by the artful practitioner—and Prof. Father José Galván, of the Pontificia Università della Santa Croce in Rome, swears by the practice. If, in his parish, a couple is in particular trouble and he has exhausted all op-

Figure 7.7. *Ethiopian coffee ceremony preparations (by Badege Bishaw ©2006. Used with permission).*

tions, he will invite them over for a *paella,* "with love and grace as central ingredients."[16]

Imagine a stakeholder's meeting, say, on a small watershed in the West, where instead of steel chairs in the City Hall or local gym as the venue with, maybe, Styrofoam coffee cups and nondairy whiteners, meetings are instead hosted alternately by constituent groups, on their turf, as described above, and each offering their cuisine. As I mentioned in chapter 4, tribal representatives in discussions on the water resources of the Columbia River invited negotiators to a First Foods Celebration, allowing them to demonstrate in a very tangible way the integration of the issues at hand with all aspects of their culture and society.[17] Now imagine following that meeting with one including a barbecue on a ranch, then a meeting including a meal of local greens hosted by environmentalists. One can visualize the profound difference in tenor that could make in discussions.

In helping to move from the physical to the emotional realms and beyond, Michelle LeBaron, a mediator and scholar of cross-cultural communications, writes of the importance of ritual, both formal and informal. In

Figure 7.8. *Volunteers in Valencia prepare a gigantic paella for "Un granito por Haiti" fundraiser after the devastating 2010 earthquake in Haiti (photo by chatani from Tokyo, Japan [CC BY 2.0, desaturated from the original], via Wikimedia Commons from Wikimedia Commons).*

her books and trainings, she is mindful of appropriate foods and spaces, as well as the social activities that precede discussions and the structure of the dialogue itself. She notes that who enters the room first, who talks first, what is talked about and for how long, and what issues will be raised and by whom, are all to be crafted artfully in a way that contributes rather than detracts.[18]

Emotional

We've noted how changing the venue or offering food thoughtfully can be very powerful, but even something as seemingly simple as introductions can be recrafted with some thought and intention. The usual method is for everyone to offer their name and some aspect of credentials—the degree or job title of each, for example—essentially developing a hierarchy of participants. Alternatively, we might draw on the use of narrative from Hinduism and introduce ourselves through stories related to the issue at hand. In my world of water conflict, initial tensions decrease palpably as stakeholders introduce themselves through some story about the watershed where they grew up or what drew them to water to begin with. One might ask participants to share the meanings of their names and why they have them, or something they wear or carry and why it is important to them. Rather than a hierarchy, we find commonalities, connections, and even the beginnings of a feeling of shared community at the end of the exercise.

Such personal and group mythologies can help us reframe the issue at hand as well. For example, for millennia the Ganges was thought too holy to be pollutable and was therefore increasingly polluted, until a focused group of local activists set about to reinvigorate the concept of "river as mother" and "purifier of us all." And thus their efforts to plant more trees to help protect the water quality gained acceptance.[19]

Framing appropriate actions for the group can likewise be drawn from calling out shared ethics. Practitioners of the Bahá'í practice of consensus, described above, for example, suggest that consensus-building can happen only in public process and that private lobbying degrades the process.

Like most faiths, Judaism has strong prohibitions against gossip: *lashon ha'rah*, literally "the evil tongue." From Matt's *Essential Kabbalah*:

> Your ears should always be tuned to hear the good, while rumors and gossip should never be let in, according to the secret of sublime listening. There, no harsh shouting enters, no tongue of evil leaves a blemish. So listen only to positive, useful things, not to things that provoke anger.

Groups of any background and culture can be reminded of their own similar precepts to help shape the tone of discussions.

Many tools can help shift emotions or help craft settings conducive to shifts. These might include the introduction of music, poetry, or gardens to the process. Barbara Miller was a manager at the well-known World Heritage Site Bahá'í Gardens in Haifa and Akko, who suggested that they were designed so that walking through them on the way to the shrines would allow one to reach them in a proper spiritual and emotional state.[20]

One of the most powerful tools at the emotional level is forgiveness, about which most faith traditions have something to contribute. At its most basic, practical level, forgiveness helps move a process forward. As is often attributed to Lily Tomlin, "Forgiveness means giving up all hope for a better past."[21] But at the deeper level, if we accept that we are all connected through our shared divinity, then healing any relationship is healing our relationship with the divine. Because under the *mable* (process of the Afar people of Ethiopia) the notion of responsibility is not conceptualized at the level of the individual but at the level of the collective, there is little difference between seeking and granting forgiveness.

Thus the Sufi practitioner Fara Gaye urges feeling others' pain and asking forgiveness "with humility and compassion."[22] On the basis of more than twenty verses in the Hebrew Bible and New Testament, Jews and Christians advocate for healing. Peacemakers Ministries, for example, offers training in conflict transformation within Evangelical communities, including a full session on forgiveness informed by, among other teachings, Colossians 3:13: "Bear with each other and forgive whatever grievances you may have against one another. Forgive as the Lord forgave you."

They suggest two aspects of forgiveness. The first, a heart component, is nonconditional, a release of an offense to God. The second component grants forgiveness conditional on genuine repentance of the offender. However, we are reminded that it is also incumbent on us to try to see our own contributions to the dispute and agree to four promises:[23]

- I will not dwell on this incident.

- I will not bring up this incident again and use it against you.

- I will not talk to others about this incident.

- I will not let this incident stand between us or hinder our personal relationships.

Ho'oponopono is an ancient Hawaiian practice of reconciliation and forgiveness, with similar practices throughout the South Pacific, that advocates four steps to the method: Repentance, Forgiveness, Gratitude, and Love.[24]

Figure 7.9. Bahá'í Gardens in Haifa (by Ariella Cohen Wolf © 2013. Used with permission).

"These are the only forces at work—but these forces have amazing power. I'm sorry, please forgive me, thank you, I love you."

On a larger scale, forgiveness has been practiced, famously in the Truth and Reconciliation processes of post-apartheid South Africa, and advocated elsewhere. In an article on the topic, Thomas Butler suggested that at the end of the hostilities in Bosnia and after the steps leading to acknowledgment and apology, "the act of forgiveness itself should be marked by a ritual to be prepared jointly by historians, poets, and musicians."[25] We've seen in chapter 2 that the ritual *sulha* has been advocated both in post–civil war Lebanon and between Israelis and Palestinians.

For those interested in more information, Fred Luskin, director and co-founder of the Stanford University Forgiveness Project, has written a very accessible text on forgiveness for individuals, *Forgive for Good*,[26] including the health and emotional benefits of the process. For the world of geopolitics, Raymond Helmick, S. J. Petersen, and Rodney Petersen edited a thorough volume on *Forgiveness and Reconciliation*,[27] with a wonderful foreword by Desmond Tutu, which includes theological roots and global applications.

The Cree Healing Circle is a process for group healing and restorative justice, which uses the Medicine Wheel and its explicit allusion to the four worlds:

> During a healing circle, an Elder might use the Medicine Wheel to explain how everyone needs to balance all four aspects in their lives. Because all four aspects are connected, if an individual concentrates on only one aspect, the other three will suffer. . . .
>
> Within Cree traditions, justice requires restoration and healing, rather than punishment or retribution. The concept of unity and wholeness of the circle is captured in the idea of holistic healing of an individual and the community at large. The circle is viewed as being whole, with no discontinuities, beginnings, or ends.
>
> Whereas mediation focuses upon what to do in the future, healing circles allow participants to consider also their history. History is an important aspect of healing in Native communities.[28]

Perceptual

In most group processes, some level of information needs to be exchanged, and volumes have been written about how best to achieve this, including communicating about really complex concepts with huge datasets (I love the work of Yale's Edward Tufte; his three volumes on data visualization are to my mind the best in the field). The reader will have no trouble finding what one needs for one's own field and situation. Recall, though, that the term *perceptual* is being used both for this intellectual exchange and for the deeper, intuitive insight that helps transform thinking and, by extension, entire processes. The tools highlighted here, then, are those that help us straddle the worlds of the intellect and intuition, often with a jolt.

Traditionally, Zen masters have used *koans* (riddles that have no logical answer, such as "What was your face before your parents were born?") and *mondos* (questions and answers that, like *koans*, defy logic). The idea

Figure 7.10. Painting from a temple depicting the Buddha stopping a war over the waters of the Rohini River (photo courtesy of Ven. Dr. Rangama Chandawimala Thero, "Kalyanamitra Dharmasabha" Google Blog Spot; used with permission).

behind these is to jolt the mind out of its habitual thought processes into *satori*, a flash of insight into the true nature of reality. The idea is to let the pure mind, "the Buddha nature within," reveal itself. Although the use of *koans* and *mondos* may be awkward to insert explicitly into our processes at work, we can certainly use the concept to encourage exercises to help jar participants from complacency and entrenched thinking.

Asking the right question at the right time can have just that impact. As I noted above, Phra Paisan Visalo, the Buddhist monk and mediator, often poses this question to effect a shift: "If you get what you are asking for, what will be the impact on the community?" He says he models his approach on that of the Buddha, who was able to stop a war with just one question (figure 7.10).

The story is that the Buddha heard about an impending war between two groups of people, the Sakiyas and the Koliyas, who had traditionally been close to each other. They were united by family ties and trade agreements, and they lived in peaceful coexistence. He started asking what the root of the conflict was, beginning at the top of the political echelon. No one seemed to know what it was about as he continued to ask down the line, only that war was imminent. Finally, when he got to the peasants, he found out it was about the waters of the Rohini River, which formed the natural border between the two states. Both groups claimed ownership of the water in the river, and when the water became scarce, they did not want to share with the other group. Returning to the leaders, he asked simply, "Is water worth more than the blood of your subjects?" And thus the war was averted.[29]

Another such approach is to explicitly encourage multiple viewpoints on an issue but also to advocate for full consensus for decision making. As I mentioned, the Bahá'ís have a fairly detailed consultation process for community decision making that encourages both. Ideas from participants are encouraged, and as they are introduced into the discussion, they are disassociated from the individual; there is no ownership. This disassociation is actually advocated as a spiritual practice; separating one's ego from one's ideas can be difficult, but it leads to richer conversations. Decisions are then made by consensus if possible, allowing continued refinement of ideas until they are acceptable to all. Albert Lincoln, who at the time was secretary-general of the Bahá'í International Community, related the process to how a river shapes stones.

> Conflicting ideas are useful to help sharpen final product. At the upper end of a stream, rocks have sharp edges, but flow (Consultation) allows them to bang together and lose the sharpness. Humility is lowest point (sea level); the entire motivation for the process.[30]

Barbarah Miller, at the time manager of the Bahá'í Gardens, described the process of "deepening" in the consultation process. If things get tense, participants will stop and read passages from the holy writings to bring back the spirit necessary to reach agreement.[31] Similarly, in some Islamic traditions, when there is a conflict between people and they approach a *kadi* (judge), he might refer them to the Koran and ask them to read relevant passages together first and see whether they can find the solution themselves.[32]

Consensus is not everyone agreeing; rather, it is no one objecting, a subtle but important distinction. The question that then is perpetually asked in order to achieve consensus is, "What would make this agreement acceptable to you?" Although reaching consensus takes time, it helps profoundly with issues of buy-in and the vulnerability that comes with power imbalance. When everyone in a process knows that they have the power to block progress, most people take the responsibility seriously and will help look for commonalities and compromise. In the end, I've found that the outliers often go along with the majority as a matter of courtesy, and just recognizing their gesture can be profound. As I mentioned, I spent 3 years as chair of the Department of Geosciences at Oregon State University, and I'm proud of the fact that in those 3 years, all decisions were made by consensus; we never took a single vote.[33]

There is a similar exercise for written agreements called the Single Text Process.[34] Common in treaty work but also applicable anywhere that a written agreement is necessary or useful, the process involves drafting a document over and over until consensus is reached. One generally writes all the text that is agreed to, leaving language in brackets around disagreements, then circling back until all the brackets are gone.

In the case of water negotiations between Israelis and Jordanians described earlier in the chapter, for example, the bracketed version would have read, "We agree mutually to recognize the [rights] [allocations] . . ." until the subsequent discussion allowed the participants to incorporate both in the new term, "rightful allocations."

Our traditions recognize the seriousness of working with text and offer guidelines for finding our deeper values within the dialogue. Talmudic study, for example, is generally done in pairs, recognizing that there are at least two legitimate ways to interpret the material. Moreover, the Talmud itself not only incorporates and documents minority opinion, it puts it first as a place of honor:

> Once, the Talmud tells us, the scholarly houses of Hillel and Shammai were locked in a dispute about the law in a particular case. For three long years the dispute went on, until finally a voice from heaven intervened. "*Eilu ve-eilu divrei Elohim chaim.* These and these are the words of the living God." The voice went on to rule in favor of Hillel, but the initial statement speaks directly to the heart of an organic view of the world. . . . This is the way God/Life operates. The organic model is not either/or; it is both/and. Life survives in the proliferation of possibilities, of viewpoints.[35]

In chapter 6, we discussed *Lectio Divina*, Divine Reading, as a Benedictine practice of a "spiritual and contemplative way to read for deeper understanding." One might read background material of participants or an agreement on which they are working with this intent, reading for positions, interests, and values, looking for common values and potential harmony.

Finally, Morihei Ueshiba, the originator of Aikido, the mind–body discipline he calls the "Art of Peace," reminds us how this perceptual level is also our link to truth, our beacon along the right path:

> In the Art of Peace, a technique can only work if it is in harmony with universal principles. Such principles need to be grasped through Mind, pure consciousness. Selfish desires thwart your progress, but Mind, not captivated by notions of victory or defeat, will liberate you. Mind fixes your senses and keeps you centered. Mind is the key to wondrous power and supreme clarity.[36]

Spiritual

Working at the spiritual level with groups can be delicate, given individuals' varied perspectives and openness to these issues. I offer these approaches in, well, the spirit in which they are intended and trust that each

Figure 7.11. Bible open to Psalms (by Josh Applegate [CC0] via https://unsplash. com/@joshapplegate).

BOX 7.1

ADAPTING *LECTIO DIVINA* FOR SINGLE-TEXT NEGOTIATIONS

As noted in chapter 6, *Lectio Divina*, Divine Reading, is a Benedictine practice of reading deeply, "from the heart," to educe holy meaning in sacred text through four steps: reading, meditation, prayer, and contemplation.[a] Martin Fowler, a lecturer in philosophy at Elon University, adapted the process for use in his philosophy classes; that exercise, to which I made minor tweaks for use in single-text negotiations, appears below.[b] Obviously, one might adapt as much or as little of this as would be comfortable in each individual setting.

Begin by having participants choose a section of the text on which either there is substantive agreement or there is substantive disagreement, for reading and meditation. (When they have more experience and confidence in the process, they can pick a passage at random and understand that choice is not integral to this exercise.) Participants try not to set a goal for how much content they will cover.

A leader prefaces the reading with a minute of group silence (Fowler uses a Tibetan singing bowl). That ensures that the mind is prepared to receive.

However, it is also important for the heart to be prepared. The participants need to care about receiving what the reading offers. One intentionally values receiving more than distractions. Electronic devices need to be kept unavailable. Each participant is silently saying that he or she is more grateful for what the words have to share than for any distractions. Gratitude allows one to be more receptive.

An individual leads the *Lectio Divina* for the class, using a suggested portion of the text. Three readings aim at different levels of receptivity to the text: being surprised, responding to the surprise, and then experiencing the surprise with new depth and insight.

1. First reading: The facilitator reads the passage aloud, slowly and carefully, sharing it with the group like unwrapping a gift.

Then comes a slow silent reading of the passage by all participants. The tempo is deliberately much slower than their usual reading. As the participants read silently, they are prepared to notice the word, phrase, sentence, or idea that captures their attention.

2. Second reading: After this time of silent reading, the facilitator reads the passage aloud once more.

Participants now meditate on the part of the text that has spoken to them. They silently repeat it, noticing what thoughts come to mind when they do so, whether it's being reminded of something or a hope. This requires patience and persistence. We have distractions between our ears too.

Not rushing ahead, but allowing time for silent reading, the facilitator then invites participants to share what has captured their attention. They are *not* called upon to explain or justify their response. The facilitator then offers the singing bowl (or some other agreed-upon talking piece) to the first participant.

When one holds the bowl, that participant has others' undivided attention and is not interrupted. If the participant does not wish to share, he or she holds the bowl in silence for ten seconds and then passes it to the next student. When responding after another participant has spoken, one shares *only* after expressing gratitude to the prior participant (by name) for what he or she has shared.

3. Third reading: The facilitator slowly and carefully reads the passage aloud to go to a deeper level. The participants silently read the passage again. In a religious context, this is called speaking to God or experiencing God's presence. The nonreligious "speaking to God" about text is not substituting speaking to oneself or speaking to others. It is practicing a mindful presence to the spirit of the gathering and how that presence (larger than and other than oneself) transforms the participant's understanding about the differences. It's letting the passage become part of who one is or wishes to become.

The participants write about their insight where they sit, including any possible ways forward. Whether they write about it religiously or nonreligiously is up to them. They may choose to share this with the group or just turn it in to the facilitator.

a. Enzo Bianchi, "Listening," Chapter 5 in Lectio Divina: From God's Word to Our Lives *(Brewster, MA: Paraclete Press, 2015).*

b. Used with permission. Fowler credits Sadhana, a Way to God: Christian Exercises in Eastern Form by the late Fr. Anthony De Mello (New York, NY: Doubleday, 1978) as an influence on his teaching.

leader or participant will judge what is appropriate for each setting and adapt accordingly.

One might be able to ease into this world with seemingly secular approaches. Music, for example, is easily introduced to many groups, yet it can have a deeper impact. Ya'qub Ibn Yusuf, a Sufi scholar in Jerusalem with background in Judaism, Buddhism, and many other faiths, notes that music gets people to breathe together, changing their rhythmic state. Recall from the last chapter that breathing together creates connection and that one can create a calming effect by breathing at the same rate as someone else, then slowing the rate of both down.

BOX 7.2

BREATHING CALM INTO THE ROOM EXERCISE

One might read this description of the Buddhist practice of projecting calm through breathing with some skepticism. So I suggest you try it.

At some point when you are triggered, perhaps by a loved one or colleague—but in a safe space, and not around an issue that evokes a trauma in your life—make a conscious effort not to respond in agitation or anger. Rather, refer back to the tools of the previous chapter: Stop, breathe, and listen. Offer to sit and hear more about what is troubling *them*. Best not to sit facing each other, but if possible at about 45 degrees (your respective gazes would cross about 5 feet in front of you). Then listen to the issue from their perspective. Don't argue, defend, or correct; listen from the heart.

As you listen, try to match their breathing rate. Don't make an overt effort, just gently note the rising and falling of their chest and lightly ease into the same rhythm. Then, just as lightly, and without losing focus of their words, softly start to ease the rhythm of your own breathing just a touch at a time.

These two simple acts—listening from the heart and sharing one's breath—have the potential to dramatically change the energy of the dialogue, and perhaps even the course of the relationship.

Edy Kaufmann, a facilitator who works with communities in crisis all over the world, notes that in group dialogues in Lesotho, a country that is about half Catholic and half Protestant, no matter how arduous a process or how deep the tensions, they will always end the day in a hymn, "in harmony!"[37]

The healing use of silence likewise can be couched in fairly secular terms as, for example, a "time-out for reflection" or "going to the balcony." Yet our traditions have exquisite models for working with silence. We can learn a lot from Quakers, for example, whose traditional meetings for worship have little or no ritual, leadership, or conversation, nor do they take turns around a circle. Rather, they sit in a silence, which they perceive as being filled with spirit. From time to time a member who feels "called" (moved from within by spirit, by their "inner light") rises and speaks. When finished, the member simply sits down. No one responds. The pregnant silence settles once more among and within the congregation.[38] Ibn Yusuf, the Sufi scholar I mentioned earlier, notes that the silent path "comes at the moment between tears and smiles."[39]

Conversely, the spoken word, with intent, can harness spiritual resonance. In the well-known *Autobiography of a Yogi*, Paramhansa Yogananda
writes,

> The infinite potencies of sound derive from the Creative Word,
> AUM, the cosmic vibratory power behind all atomic energies. Any
> word spoken with clear realization and deep concentration has a
> materializing value. Loud or silent repetition of inspiring words
> has been found effective in Coueism and similar systems of psy-
> chotherapy; the secret lies in the stepping-up of the mind's vibra-
> tory rate.[40]

Subbappa and Michele Ribeiro help elucidate AUM, explaining that
it is the sound chanted that activates the elements of nature within the
physical attributes of the body. A is chanted from the space of the abdo-
men, which influences the elements of water, earth, and fire. U resonates
in the chest, which influences the element of air. M resonates from the
throat and above, influencing space/ether, which encompasses mind/
consciousness. Glen Hearns adds that the silence after AUM is as much a
part as that which is audible. This is represented by the dot on the top of
the AUM symbol, called *turiya*, which combines all other states and transcends them to the state of full awareness.[41]

Similarly, Morihei Ueshiba writes,

> All sounds and vibrations emanated from that Word (*su*). Your
> voice is a very powerful weapon. When you are in tune with the cos-
> mic breath of heaven and earth, your voice produces true sounds.
> Unify body, mind, and speech, and real techniques will emerge.[42]

The United Methodist Church's Center for Mediation and Conflict
Transformation produced a document called *Engage Conflict Well*,[43] which
draws on Christian ethics and approaches to transform conflict. In a section called "Drink Deeply Together," they draw on the power of language,
noting how positive and elevating words are self-reinforcing, so starting
on that note is crucial; sharing stories of peak experiences generates energy for moving forward:

- Be intentional about starting the process with remembering and telling stories of positive experiences or moments of grace.

- Starting with such stories is usually the better place to start than with the negative stories and a problem-solving approach. In the context of such stories, the problems can then be addressed more easily and more constructively.

They suggest that the most powerful tool in this process is an open-ended, positive question:

- Take the time and care to craft questions that evoke the positive experiences, dreams, and constructive responses, such as "What are your hopes for this meeting?" instead of "What are the problems that have brought you here?"

- Positive questions promote the forward momentum of a good process; for example, "If your hopes for our meeting are fulfilled, what will our world, our community, and our relationships look like?"

- In the sacred space of conflict, remembering grace-filled moments and expressing dreams of a preferred future, the primary question is always, "What is God's love calling us to be and to do?"

$\sim$

Finally, if the setting is right, one might actually tap prayer explicitly. Often in my work in a variety of situations around the world, inviting one religious leader to open a meeting in prayer could be extremely divisive, yet inviting several has the opposite, elevating effect. I have noted in meetings with Arabs and Israelis, for example, that on the occasions that Christian, Muslim, and Jewish leaders have all opened with a prayer and some reflection of what water means in their tradition, the conversations tend to ease more readily into shared values and harmony rather than starting with divisive positions. Likewise, in the Wwestern United States I have been to several meetings opened by spiritual leaders from the tribe on whose land we are meeting, creating a similar elevating impact.

$\sim$

BOX 7.3

RIGHT SPEECH AND THREE THINGS

Right Speech is the third factor in Buddhism's Eightfold Path. The *Vaca Sutta* explains that a well-spoken statement has five characteristics. It is spoken at the right time. It is spoken in truth. It is spoken affectionately. It is spoken beneficially. It is spoken with a mind of good will. Of course, knowing when *not* to speak can be an equally powerful spiritual practice. Questions one might ask before speaking based on right speech, then, would include:

- Is it timely?
- Is it true?
- Is the intention healing?
- Is it kind?
- Will it be received?

A more prosaic source, comedian Craig Ferguson, urges that everyone should ask themselves three questions before opening their mouths:

1. Does this need to be said?
2. Does this need to be said by me?
3. Does this need to be said by me *now*?

Think how much better the world would run if everyone followed this sage advice.

Sources: Vaca Sutta translated from the Pali by Thanissaro Bhikkhu, http://www.accesstoinsight.org/tipi taka/an/an05/an05.198.than.html; Craig Ferguson, "Does This Need to Be Said?" Online video clip (Comedy Central, October 7, 2011. http://www.cc.com/video-clips/2499vl/stand-up-craig-ferguson—uncensored —does-this-need-to-be-said-).

If one is tasked, one might then pull together the lessons of the last chapter and integrate with this structure to help us in designing more effective processes for groups:

1. Craft a topic for discussion that is based on shared values (*ands*, not *ors*, for example).

2. Think of the positions, interests, and values of the parties who will be in the room and, again, plan on leading the discussion from values.

3. Design a map, either together with participants or for your own use, that shows the connections of both the system under discussion and the relationships of the participants.

Figure 7.12. *First Foods Festival dinner (by Columbia River Inter-Tribal Fish Commission, used with permission).*

4. Design a process that addresses the physical, emotional, perceptual, and spiritual needs of the people in the room, recognizing that the process may well wend and meander through the group expressions of the ARIA model.

~

So let's come back to the "cowboys" and "tree-huggers" from the Bureau of Reclamation–led meeting described at the start of the chapter. After we had separated out the bureau staff and sent the others off on a field trip, I was quite transparent that not only were their internal tensions palpable but because they represented the host agency, we could not move the process forward to "integration" or "action" until they themselves had moved past "antagonism" at least to "reflexive."

So I opened up some time for venting about what each participant saw as the source of discord within their office. As often happens, despite my prompt asking each to reflect on their own internal concerns and what each might contribute to salving the situation, what came out instead was a torrent of accusations, tinged with a bit of mythic story. One side accused the other of both literally and figuratively bulldozing through both structures and processes, building without concern for the environment, and moving forward without concern for dialogue. In turn, that side was accused of ignoring the benefits that building brings and of caring more for nature than for people.

Jay Rothman, who developed the ARIA model, describes in his 2012 text some rich exercises designed to help groups move especially from antagonism to reflection, one of which is simply to ask participants to role play as someone with whom they disagree. He describes the transformative moment in an Arab–Israeli dialogue outside Jerusalem when a Palestinian Arab started to describe what he, in role, saw as an "Israeli Jew." There are few better ways to show that one really has absorbed what the "other" is trying to express than to express it for them.

So the "cowboys" became the "tree-huggers" and vice versa. This not only showed that underneath the bluster and rhetoric there really was a certain amount of empathy for each side but also drew out some well-needed humor and good-natured ribbing. One participant in his role as an environmental regulator jokingly expressed his philosophy as "BANANA: build absolutely nothing anywhere near anything."

What become clear in the exchange was how the Bureau of Reclamation had changed over the years in response to changing societal values. From its creation in 1902 through the 1970s, the mandate was to help irrigate the West, which pretty much meant building stuff: massive dams such as Hoover on the Colorado and Grand Coulee on the Columbia and thousands of others, along with immense canalways and drainage projects throughout the U.S. West. Their engineers had a can-do attitude and a clear mission to make the arid portions of the country livable and productive.

The decrease in available and tenable dam and irrigation sites coincided in the 1970s with a growing environmental awareness and legislative requirements. Brakes were applied to the "get 'er done" approach, and the bureau adapted procedures to help protect the environment and incorporate public participation in decision making. This evolution resulted in real splits in many of their area offices, with a construction side often at odds with the environmental side. In parallel, these splits were defined not only by mission—one to build and one to protect—but also by age, with the former group generally older, and by diversity, the latter being generally more diverse both racially and by gender.

All of this played into the divisions in our meeting. As each participant in role described the issues as seen through the eyes of the "other," it became clear that not only did each side understand each other, but there was actually deep respect for what the other side did. This was critically important, especially for the construction side, to hear. Recall from earlier the role that vulnerability plays in fostering anger and conflict. And from the construction side, it became apparent that underlying their frustration was the view that everything they built was under attack, as was the motivation for their entire life's work.

A turning point came as one "tree-hugger" expressed her gratitude to the others: "Every time I turn on the lights or grab something in the fridge, I appreciate what you guys do for us day in and day out."

From the place of empathy and respect, it was fairly straightforward to build a unified approach to hosting the dialogue as a whole. "Let's face it," one participant encouraged, "we have all sides represented right here in our office, and if we can figure it out, who better to lead the group as a whole?"

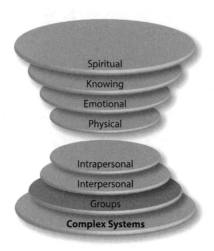

Figure 8.1.

Figure 8.2. *A moment of joy (photo by photo-nic.co.uk nic [CC0], via https://
unsplash.com/@chiro).*

CHAPTER EIGHT

A Leap of Faith:
Complexity and Conflict

You must be the change you want to see in the world.

—Mahatma Gandhi

Initially, I had thought to include a chapter on complex systems, but as I got here, I realized I have little to offer at that scale. This book is about how we might transform conflict, and at the scale of systems, we have little apparent impact. I say "apparent" because I believe firmly that, as our faith traditions teach, all we can do is do what we can, and have faith that collectively it will make a difference.

As the system we are attempting to understand grows in scale and complexity, our understanding of how to affect the system, especially in a positive direction, drops dramatically. This is especially true when dealing with complex scientific issues. In my part of the world, the salmon population in the Columbia River basin has dropped precipitously as dams and development have taken hold over the decades. Although we know there is a rough inverse relationship between development and fish, we can't point to reasonable specific actions that will definitively bring them back to historic levels. Same with most of the major issues of the day, such as climate change.

So we develop management techniques that allow us to learn as we incrementally move forward, such as "adaptive management," or "managing through intention," and craft principles such as the "precautionary principle" that we hope at least won't allow us to fall too far backwards.[1]

And, most critically, we do what we can in our own little microcatch-ment and pray that it scales up.

So too with conflict.

We start with our internal disputes and, through learning to heal those, learn something about healing our relationships with others. Then we move forward in faith that having healthier conversations with other individuals and within small groups will have a cumulative effect and scale up. Or so we pray.

~

Again, I am at heart a scientist and a utilitarian. This exploration is simply about enhancing the toolbox of anyone facilitating dialogue at different levels. I come to this material because it works, and has worked for thou-sands of years. Good scientists go where the evidence leads them, with-out preconceptions or artificial boundaries. The rift between science and transcendence rent by the Enlightenment is just such an artificial bound-ary, but as our problems become larger and more complex, so must our approaches to resolving and transforming them.

I leave the last word on the topic to Reb Zalman Schachter-Shalomi, of blessed memory, whose lecture on the four worlds as understood in a variety of spiritual traditions so inspired me long ago, and who has thought deeply about our relationships to each other, to the earth, and to the divine:

> Religion and spirituality have too often been at war with science
> and modernity, but these and these are the diverse expressions of a
> living God. Each needs the other. A religion that stands only as the
> champion of the past will sooner or later cease to speak to us. But
> science needs spirit as well. Our faith connects us to the unknow-
> able mystery that will always be at the heart of the scientific en-
> deavor. We need the deep wisdom of the ancients to comfort and
> inspire us as we grapple with issues that are new and potentially
> very frightening. A science without both love and reverence is a
> cold endeavor indeed—and potentially dangerous as well. Finally
> leaps of faith and intuition can take us to the places where science
> cannot yet go.[2]

BOX 8.1

RE-TRAVELING THE FOUR WORLDS EXERCISE

Let's take another look at the four worlds exercise from chapter 3 (box 3.5, p. 50) and see what we've learned. Here's the setup:

You'll need a friend to help you with this, ideally someone who is articulate and can act passionately about ideas. And definitely someone you trust.

Sit with your friend in a quiet location where you won't disturb anyone. Close off distractions and turn off your phone. Now, choose a topic of current events, something that you feel very strongly about (but *not* one that has even the slightest possibility of evoking personal trauma in your life). Which side of the issue do you identify with?

Now, ask your friend to argue as passionately as possible, taking the opposite position. But here's the trick: You are not allowed to say a word for 4 full minutes. Just listen. But try to really listen, even though it will be hard. Even though your friend may not (or, if he or she is your friend, probably does not) believe in the position they are taking, encourage them to argue it as forcefully and as clearly as possible.

As you listen, try to also notice carefully what's going on inside you.

∼

Recall that, at the time, and before reading this far in the book, chances are you moved energetically through the four worlds, starting with intense physical discomfort, followed by emotions such as anger or agitation.

Then, as you continued to listen, here's what was suggested in chapter 3:

Next might come something both surprising and interesting. If you're really listening—*really* listening—you might at some point actually feel a palpable shift in your perception. As you hear difficult ideas so clearly articulated, some part of you might relax the defenses of your physical and emotional shields enough to be intellectually curious about the other side and the beginnings of a readiness to intuit connections between what you thought existed only as two mutually exclusive sides. You'll feel this shift up around your head, but vaguely.

Most people's experience will stop somewhere in the first two or three levels. But if you're willing to lose yourself to the experience, and if you have practice focusing acutely—maybe you pray or run or fish or meditate—you might have a brief, ethereal sense of connection, not just with the ideas and your friend, but with the broader universe of all ideas and all friends. If you feel this at all, it might actually feel as if it is happening outside your physical body, perhaps just above and in front of you (although not quite).

∼

continued

Box 8.1 *continued*

Now see if you can find a way to redo the exercise, either as a simulation or, if you are brave, engage someone with whom you disagree on an issue, and ask them to explain their perspective while you listen. Is the experience any different now that you have a broader sense of context? Is the energy moving up any less painfully?

Recall from chapter 6 how a situation can be instantly changed with the right question. Here are two that might be useful as you engage in difficult conversations, both in this exercise and in your life:

1. As you start to feel the physical and emotional discomfort, use it as a signal to ask yourself this question: "Is there anything I can learn in this situation?"

This simple question can help shift you into listening mode and will help profoundly in moving the energy upward to the perceptual level and decreasing the physical and emotional discomfort at the same time.

2. The second question can be formed internally as you are listening: "What do I share with this person?" How you picture this depends on your personal theology; when I say "share" I mean in a spiritual sense. Can you picture the light of the divine in the person you are listening to, regardless of his or her views? Is there a way to comfortably visualize your shared holiness? Try.

This question moves the energy from the perceptual state to the spiritual and will probably change the tenor of the discussion at the very least. It could end up changing your relationship as well.

Figure 8.3. Kabbalah Mandala *(painting by Paul Heussenstamm, mandalas .com; used with permission).*

Notes

Chapter 1

1. Anyone interested in what we did find can obtain the meeting report at the website for the Program in Water Conflict Management and Transformation (PWCMT) at Oregon State University (http://www.transboundarywaters.orst.edu).
2. In the next chapter, I will talk more about scholars who actually have been instrumental in introducing energy work and the transformative moment into ADR more recently.

Chapter 2

1. See David Martin, "The religious and the secular: Pressure points and alignments," (keynote address, Forum 2000, Prague, October 8, 2007), for a good summary of the evolution of the Enlightenment.
2. See, for example, T. P. O'Connor, J. Duncan, and F. Quillard, "Criminology and religion: The shape of an authentic dialogue," *The Journal of Criminology & Public Policy 5*, no. 3 (2006): 559–570.
3. Benedict XVI, citing John 1:1, in "Lecture of the Holy Father: Faith, Reason and the University Memories and Reflections," *Libreria Editrice Vaticana*, September 12, 2006, accessed November 26, 2016, http://w2.vatican.va/content/benedict-xvi/en/speech es/2006/september/documents/hf_ben-xvi_spe_20060912_university-regensburg .html.
4. Prof. James V. Schall, in his 2007 commentary on the lecture, suggests, "In the Catholic tradition, faith was not a rival to or alternative to reason. . . . Reason had to be reason if revelation is to be revelation. Revelation is not an escape from reason nor a denial of it. It is a stimulus to it in its own depths." James V. Schall, *The Regensburg Lecture* (South Bend, IN: St. Augustine's Press, 2007), 96.
5. Laurence Khantipālo Mills, *Buddhism Explained* (Chiang Mai, Thailand: Silkworm Books, 1999), 2.
6. Huston Smith, *The World's Religions: Our Great Wisdom Traditions*. San Francisco: HarperSanFrancisco, 1991 (rev. and updated ed. of *The Religions of Man*, 1958), 96.
7. For accessible introductions to Kabbalah, see Gershom Scholem, *On the Kabbalah and Its Symbolism* (New York: Schocken Books, 1965); Daniel C. Matt, *The Essential Kabbalah: The Heart of Jewish Mysticism* (Edison, NJ: Castle Books, 1997); and Arthur Green, *Ehyeh: A Kabbalah for Tomorrow* (Nashville, TN: Jewish Lights Publishing, 2004).
8. *Justice* is meant here in the strict, bounded sense and is not meant in the same vein as one might refer to a more holistic restorative justice.
9. For a history, see Don Karr, "The Study of Christian Cabala in English," *Hermetic Kabbalah*, 2016. http://www.digital-brilliance.com/contributed/Karr/Biblios/ccinea .pdf. On nuance, my friend and colleague (and Christian) Kim Ogren notes, "We view God as both just and merciful, and the themes and balance of justice, mercy, and

compassion are very present in Christianity. It is through Jesus Christ that there is both justice served (his death as atonement) and mercy given (to all who accept it)."

10. Khaled Abou El Fadl, *Islam and the Challenge of Democracy* (Princeton, NJ: Princeton University Press, 2004).

11. Bahá'í Administration, A selection of letters and messages addressed to the Bahá'ís of the United States and Canada, written between January 1922 and July 1932, p. 45, available at http://www.bahai.org/library/authoritative-texts/shoghi-effendi/bahai-administration/.
    More directly, 'Abdu'l-Bahá, writes in *The Promulgation of Universal Peace*: "The third principle or teaching of Bahá'u'lláh is the oneness of religion and science. Any religious belief which is not conformable with scientific proof and investigation is superstition, for true science is reason and reality, and religion is essentially reality and pure reason; therefore, the two must correspond. Religious teaching which is at variance with science and reason is human invention and imagination unworthy of acceptance, for the antithesis and opposite of knowledge is superstition born of the ignorance of man. If we say religion is opposed to science, we lack knowledge of either true science or true religion, for both are founded upon the premises and conclusions of reason, and both must bear its test" (p. 107).

12. One could easily see the same structure in the triumvirates of id, ego, and superego, or thesis, antithesis, synthesis.

13. Ly Trong Tinh, personal communication, 2008.

14. As Pope Benedict did with such controversy in the Regensburg Lecture in 2006. Benedict XVI, "Lecture of the Holy Father: Faith, Reason and the University Memories and Reflections," *Libreria Editrice Vaticana*, September 12, 2006, accessed November 26, 2016, http://w2.vatican.va/content/benedict-xvi/en/speeches/2006/september/documents/hf_ben-xvi_spe_20060912_university-regensburg.html.

15. Manfred Halpern left an unfinished manuscript on the topic as his Princeton class notes for Politics 325, published posthumously as *Transforming the Personal, Political, Historical and Sacred in Theory and Practice* (Scranton, PA: University of Scranton Press, 2009), 47.

16. Harvard Negotiation Insight Initiative, "Launching Document," (unpublished manuscript, 2003). http://www.pon.harvard.edu/tag/harvard-negotiation-institute/.

17. Heidi Burgess, "Transformative Mediation: A Summary" (Boulder, CO: University of Colorado Conflict Research Consortium, 1997). http://www.colorado.edu/conflict/transform/tmall.htm.

18. Carol Hwoschinsky, "Listening to the Heart," *Alternatives* 25 (Spring 2003).

19. Uzi Weingarten, "Communicating with Compassion," course notes from online class taught by Bernard Uzi Weingarten in 2003. Course now offered at http://uziteaches.com/.

20. Abou El Fadl, p. 54.

21. John A. McConnell, *Mindful Mediation: A Handbook for Buddhist Peacemakers* (Bangkok, Thailand: Buddhist Research Institute, 1995).

22. Trip Barthel, "Unity and Diversity in Conflict Resolution," *ACResolution* 5, no. 1 (Fall 2005), 32.

23. As Eileen Barker, Chair of the ACR Spirituality Section, asks in her introductory article, "How can we 'be the peace' we wish to create for others?" See Eileen Barker, "What the BLEEP Does Spirituality Have to Do with Conflict Resolution?" *ACResolution* 5, no. 1 (Fall 2005): 10–11.

24. Leonard L. Riskin, "The Contemplative Lawyer: On the Potential Contributions of Mindfulness Meditation to Law Students, Lawyers, and their Clients," *Harvard Negotiation Law Review* 7, no. 1 (Spring 2002): 1–67; Daniel Bowling, "Who Am I as a Mediator? Mindfulness, Reflection and Presence," *ACResolution* 5, no. 1 (Fall 2005): 12–15.

25. See Kenneth Cloke, "Why Every Conflict Breaks Your Heart: Conflict as a Spiritual Crisis," *ACResolution* 5, no. 1 (Fall 2005): 16–21; and Mark Umbreit, "Mindfulness, Deep Listening and Stories: The Spiritual Core of Peacemaking," *ACResolution* 5, no. 1 (Fall 2005): 26–27.

26. Notably, Leonard L. Riskin, "Mindfulness: Foundational Training for Dispute Resolution," *Journal of Legal Education* 4, no. 1 (March 2004): 79–90; Erica Ariel Fox and Mark Gafni, "Seeing with New Eyes: One Step Toward the Field of the Future," *ACResolution* 5, no. 1 (Fall 2005): 22–25; and Kenneth Cloke, *The Crossroads of Conflict: A Journey into the Heart of Dispute Resolution* (Calgary, Alberta: Janis, 2006).

27. Marc Gopin, *Between Eden and Armageddon: The Future of World Religions, Violence, and Peacemaking* (Oxford: Oxford University Press, 2000).

28. Anyone interested in what I learned can find the results here: A. Wolf, "Indigenous Approaches to Water Conflict Negotiations and Implications for International Waters," *International Negotiation: A Journal of Theory and Practice* 5, no. 2 (December 2000): 357–373.

29. As Fara Gaye, a Sufi master from Senegal, told me succinctly in 2004, "Spirituality unites, while religion divides" (personal communication).

30. For those who would like more extensive and nuanced definitions of these concepts, I highly recommend Arthur J. Schwartz, "The Nature of Spiritual Transformation: A Review of the Literature" (unpublished manuscript, fall 2000), available at: http://www.metanexus.net/archive/spiritualtransformationresearch/research/pdf/STSRP-LiteratureReview2-7.PDF; Peter J. Jankowski, "Postmodern Spirituality: Implications for Promoting Change," *Counseling and Values* 47, no. 1 (October 2002): 69–79; and Frederic Luskin, "Transformative Practices for Integrating Mind–Body–Spirit," *The Journal of Alternative and Complementary Medicine* 10 (Supplement 1, 2004): S15–23.

31. In a 2013 conversation on the topic, Swami Subodhananda of the Chinmaya Ashram at Sidhbari, India asked me rhetorically, "We don't say geography is a source of war, do we?" (personal communication).

32. O'Connor, Duncan, and Quillard, "Criminology and Religion."

33. Elias Jabbour, *Sulha: Palestinian Traditional Peacemaking Process* (Montreat, NC: House of Hope Publications, 1993, 1996).

34. See Daniel L. Smith, "The Rewards of Allah," *Journal of Peace Research* 26, no. 4 (1989): 385–398; Jabbour, *Sulha*; and George Irani, "Islamic Mediation Techniques for Middle East Conflicts," *Middle East Review of International Affairs (MERIA) Journal* 3, no. 2 (June 1999): n.p., for more detail.

35. Jabbour, *Sulha*, 116.

36. To some degree, this concept is being introduced in some larger contexts in the Middle East. Irani, "Islamic Mediation Techniques," describes a *sulha* that was carried out between the Christian and Muslim communities in Beirut. The interviewees in Smith, "Rewards of Allah," argue that although the problems between Israelis and Palestinians are too great to be dealt with in a simple ceremony, the principles of *sulha*, balancing rights with honor, might be applied. H. Tarabeih, D. Shmueli, and R. Khamaisi, in "Towards the Implementation of Sulha as a Cultural Peacemaking Method for Managing and Resolving Environmental Conflicts among Arab Palestinians in Israel," *Journal*

of Peacebuilding and Development 5, no. 1 (2009): 50–64, similarly suggest the *sulha* as a potential vehicle for Jewish and Muslim Israeli environmental dialogue.

37. Steve MacAusland, quoted in Anonymous. "Massachusetts Episcopal Diocese Bases Reorganization on Watersheds," *Earthkeeping News* 5, no. 6 (September/October 1996), 1–2.

Chapter 3

1. Described by R. Bachya Ben Asher, a Spanish commentator (1263–1340) who first applied the four worlds into a Torah commentary, based on four simultaneous yet sequential levels of meaning of text: plain, *midrashic* (*aggadic* or homiletic), philosophical, and Kabbalistic exegesis. See R. Bachya ben Asher, *Midrash Rabbeinu Bachya*, first published in 1492; currently available in English and Hebrew as *Rabbeinu Bachya: Commentary on the Torah*. New York: Judaica Press, 1998, seven volumes.

2. Exodus 19:16–25 (ArtScroll Chumash, Stone Edition. New York: Mesorah Publications, 1993).

3. Exodus 24:11 (ArtScroll Chumash).

4. Notably Onkelos (c. 90 CE) and the Ramban (R. Moshe ben Nachman, 1194–1270). See R. Nosson Scherman, ed., *The Stone Edition Chumash* (New York: Mesorah Publications, 1993, revised 2001), 443.

5. Exodus 24:12 (ArtScroll Chumash).

6. Eleanor Mannikka, *Angkor: Celestial Temples of the Khmer Empire* (New York: Abbeville Press, 2002), cited in Jarus, Owen. "Angkor Wat: History of Ancient Temple." *LiveScience* (October 8, 2014). http://www.livescience.com/23841-angkor-wat.html.

7. Scherman, *Stone Edition Chumash*, 405.

8. In Jewish mysticism, they are seen in Kabbalah in the worlds of *Assiyah* (action), *Yetzirah* (formation), *Beriyah* (creation), and *Atzilut* (emanation), each with its element: earth, water, air, and fire, respectively. See Daniel C. Matt, *The Essential Kabbalah: The Heart of Jewish Mysticism* (Edison, NJ: Castle Books, 1997), for more information.

9. According to some traditions, each Sight occurred on a different day.

10. Laurence Khantipālo Mills, *Buddhism Explained* (Chiang Mai, Thailand: Silkworm Books, 1999); Walpola Rahula, *What the Buddha Taught*. Kindle edition (New York: Grove Press, 2007).

11. Four Jhannas: levels achieved in Buddhist meditation that correspond to "the four great levels of the heavenly realm," as noted in Mills, *Buddhism Explained*, 103.

12. Continuous flow of the cycle of life.

13. Ven. Mahathera Nauyane Ariyadhamma, "Anapana Sati: Meditation on Breathing" (1994) in *A Theravada Library* at Access to Insight, 2005. Available at: http://www .accesstoinsight.org/lib/authors/ariyadhamma/bl115.html.

14. Buddhadāsa Bhikkhu. *ānāpānasati: Mindfulness with Breathing: Unveiling the Secrets of Life*. Chaiya, Thailand: Dhammadāna Foundation, 1988.

15. Three of the five conflicting tribes in the oasis of Yathrib, to which Mohammed fled from Mecca, and which later became Medina, were Jewish. Mohammed had extensive experience with the community, including uniting them for a time through mediation, before relations soured and became embroiled in the politics of the day.

16. Swami Tejomayananda, *Hindu Culture* (Mumbai, India: Chinmaya Mission West, 1993), 49.

17. Both Jewish and Muslim mystical schools reached great heights together in the thirteenth century (Prof. Jon Katz, personal communication, 2015).

18. Huston Smith, *The World's Religions: Our Great Wisdom Traditions* (San Francisco, CA: HarperSanFrancisco, 1991), 261. See also Sheikh Ragip Robert Frager al Jerrahi, *Introduction to Essential Sufism*, ed. James Fadiman and Robert Frager (San Francisco: HarperSanFrancisco, 1999), 1–31; Ibn Yusuf, personal communication, 2005.

19. A project by a Native American intertribal group to compile and spread teachings common to tribes and First Nations of the Americas. See the Four Worlds International Institute: http://www.fwii.net.

20. Julie Bopp et al., *Sacred Tree: Reflections on Native American Spirituality* (Twin Lakes, WI: Lotus Press, 1984), 9.

21. Bopp et al. *Sacred Tree*, 12.

22. Alberto Villoldo, *The Four Insights: Wisdom, Power, and Grace of the Earthkeepers.* (Carlsbad, CA: Hay House, Inc., 2006).

23. Villoldo, *The Four Insights*, 6.

24. Rabbi Zalman Schachter-Shalomi, with Joel Segel. *Jewish with Feeling: A Guide to Meaningful Jewish Practice* (New York: Riverhead Books, 2005).

25. Villoldo, *The Four Insights*.

26. Through the reptilian, limbic, cortex, and "unused" portions of our brain, respectively.

27. Huston Smith, *Forgotten Truth: The Common Vision of the World's Religions* (New York: HarperCollins, 1976), 34.

28. *Pardes* translates from the Hebrew to "orchard" and it is also an acronym for *P'shat*, literal; *Remez*, hinted at; *D'rash*, homiletic; and *Sod*, secret.

29. Matt, *The Essential Kabbalah*.

30. Described in *English Translation of the Catechism of the Catholic Church* (United States Catholic Conference, Inc. 1997), paragraphs 115–119. http://www.catholicculture.org/culture/library/catechism/. Roots have been described as going back to Origen, who in turn applied Plato's threefold distinction—body, soul, and spirit—to text. Augustine refined the distinction to four: history, analogy, allegory, and etiology. See Bill Burns, "The Four Senses of Scripture," *Is My Phylactery Showing?* (blog post, May 16, 2007). http://theocoid.blogspot.com/2007/05/four-senses-of-scripture.html.

31. U.S. Catholic Conference, *Catechism*.

32. See note 8 for more information on the Kabbalistic notions of four worlds and the divine consciousness.

33. Matt, *The Essential Kabbalah*.

34. Jay Rothman, "Supplementing Tradition: A Theoretical and Practical Typology for International Conflict Management," *Negotiation Journal* 5, no. 3 (1989).

35. C. Otto Scharmer, *Theory U: Leading from the Future as It Emerges: The Social Technology of Presencing* (Cambridge, MA: Society for Organizational Learning, 2007).

36. Ken Wilber, *A Theory of Everything: An Integral Vision for Business, Politics, Science, and Spirituality* (Boston: Shambhala, 2000).

Chapter 4
1. Swami Vivekananda, *The Complete Works of Swami Vivekananda, Volume 7, Conversations and Dialogues* (1907 [original publication date]). On *Wikisource*: https://en.wikisource.org/w/index.php?title=The_Complete_Works_of_Swami_Vivekananda/Volume_7/Conversations_And_Dialogues&oldid=4900933 (accessed December 16, 2016).

2. Alberto Villoldo, *The Four Insights: Wisdom, Power, and Grace of the Earthkeepers* (Carlsbad, CA: Hay House, 2006).

3. Caroline Myss, *Anatomy of the Spirit: The Seven Stages of Power and Healing* (New York: Three Rivers Press, 1996).

4. Myss, *Anatomy of the Spirit*, 79.

5. Daniel C. Matt, *The Essential Kabbalah: The Heart of Jewish Mysticism* (Edison, NJ: Castle Books, 1997), 48–49.

6. Villoldo, *The Four Insights*, 21.

7. In a concert once, folk singer Arlo Guthrie reportedly commented that songs come to him fully formed, as if he plucked them out of a stream. He joked that he thanks God every day that he is not downstream of Bob Dylan. There are numerous variations on the "fishing" story, including a version told by Dylan himself during an interview: see Paul Zollo, *Songwriters on Songwriting* (Boston: Da Capo Press, 2003), 71.

8. Jay Rothman, "Supplementing Tradition: A Theoretical and Practical Typology for International Conflict Management," *Negotiation Journal* 5, no. 3 (1989).

9. Jay Rothman, initially described his stages as ARI—adversarial, reflexive, and integrative—in Rothman, "Supplementing Tradition." When ARI became ARIA, adding action, Rothman's terminology also evolved to antagonism, resonance, invention, and action. See Jay Rothman, *Resolving Identity-Based Conflicts in Nations, Organizations, and Communities* (San Francisco: Jossey-Bass, 1997). I retain the former terms, thinking they are more descriptive for our purposes.

10. See Matt, *The Essential Kabbalah*, and other Kabbalistic sources for the dissipation of the final distinction, that between *'ein*, "nothingness," and *ein sof*, "that which is without end." In very crude, theologically inaccurate terms, this might be thought of as the dissipation of the distinction between "nothing is God" and "everything is God." With perfect understanding, one could hold that there is no difference between these two concepts.

11. This nondual understanding of the universe is found broadly beyond the Kabbalistic, Sufi, and Toltec examples mentioned here, in, for example, Swami Tejomayananda's (1993) description of the "first and absolute aspect of Deity as the nameless, formless, and attributeless Reality, the origin of this creation" (p. 49), or in the Taoist understanding of the ultimate erasure between yin and yang (Phra Paisan Visalo, personal communication, 2005).
Paramahansa Yogananda nicely describes the relationship between matter and consciousness in his well-known *Autobiography of a Yogi* (New York: The Philosophical Library, Inc., 1946, e-book): "The different sensory stimuli to which man reacts—tactual, visual, gustatory, auditory, and olfactory—are produced by vibratory variations in electrons and protons. The vibrations in turn are regulated by 'lifetrons,' subtle life forces or finer-than-atomic energies intelligently charged with the five distinctive sensory idea-substances."

12. Don Miguel Ruiz, *The Four Agreements: A Practical Guide to Personal Freedom* (San Rafael, CA: Amber-Allen Publishing, 1997), xvii.

13. Sheikh Ragip Robert Frager Al-Jerrahi, *Introduction to Essential Sufism*, ed. James Fadiman and Robert Frager (San Francisco: HarperSanFrancisco, 1999), 13.

Chapter 5

1. Alberto Villoldo, *The Four Insights: Wisdom, Power, and Grace of the Earthkeepers* (Carlsbad, CA: Hay House, 2006), 21.

2. Articles are as follows: Eileen Barker, "What the BLEEP Does Spirituality Have to Do with Conflict Resolution?" *ACResolution* 5, no. 1 (Fall 2005), 10–11; Daniel Bowling,

"Who Am I as a Mediator? Mindfulness, Reflection and Presence," *ACResolution* 5, no. 1 (Fall 2005), 12–15; Kenneth Cloke, "Why Every Conflict Breaks Your Heart: Conflict as a Spiritual Crisis," *ACResolution* 5, no. 1 (Fall 2005), 16–21; Erica Ariel Fox and Marc Gafni, "Seeing with New Eyes: One Step Toward the Field of the Future," *ACResolution* 5, no. 1 (Fall 2005), 22–25; Mark Umbreit, "Mindfulness, Deep Listening and Stories: The Spiritual Core of Peacemaking," *ACResolution* 5, no. 1 (Fall 2005), 26–27; and Tom Fisher, "Beginner's Mind: Cultivating Mediator Mindfulness." *ACResolution* 5, no. 1 (Fall 2005), 28–29.

3. See Leonard L. Riskin, "Mindfulness: Foundational Training for Dispute Resolution," *Journal of Legal Education* 4, no. 1 (March 2004), 79–90.

4. Scott Rodgers, *The Mindful Mediator: Embracing the Uncertainty of Conflict.* http://the mindfulmediator.com/about.html.

5. Daniel Bowling and David A. Hoffman, *Bringing Peace into the Room: How the Personal Qualities of the Mediator Impact the Process of Conflict Resolution* (San Francisco: Jossey-Bass, 2003).

6. Erica Ariel Fox, *Winning from Within: A Breakthrough Method for Leading, Living, and Lasting Change* (New York: Harper Business, 2013).

7. See J. Carrera, *Inside the Yoga Sutras: A Comprehensive Sourcebook for the Study and Practice of Patanjali's Yoga Sutras* (Buckingham, VA: Integral Yoga Publications, 2006).

8. Anthony Mottola, trans., *The Spiritual Exercises of Saint Ignatius* (New York, NY: Bantam, 1964).

9. David O. McKay, *Conference Reports* (April 1967): 85, cited in Philip G. McLemore, "Mormon Mantras: A Journey of Spiritual Transformation," *Sunstone Magazine* (April 2006), 20–31.

10. Described, for example, in both Thich Nhat Hanh, *Transformation & Healing: Sutra on the Four Establishments of Mindfulness* (Berkeley, CA: Parallax Press, 1990); and Nhâit Haònh and Annabel Laity, *The Sutra on the Full Awareness of Breathing: With Commentary by Thich Nhat Hanh* (Berkeley, CA: Parallax Press, 1988), both of which have been translated and annotated by Thich Nhat Hanh (1990 and 1988, respectively). There is a clear "manual for serious beginners" for practice of the latter, by Buddhadã Bhikkhu, translated by Santikaro Bhikkhu, called *Mindfulness with Breathing: A Manual for Serious Beginners* (Bangkok: The Dhamma Study & Practice Group, with help from Evolution/Liberation, 1988), available online, http://www.dhammatalks.net/Books3/Bhikkhu_Buddhadasa_Anapanasati_Mindfulness_with_Breathing.htm.

11. Mark McCrea, workshop and personal communications, July 2010.

12. McLemore, *Mormon Mantras*, 21.

13. Jerome Delli Priscoli, personal communication, Rome, 2004.

14. Jerome Delli Priscoli, "Christology and Faith Experience of Dispute Resolution and Collaborative Problem Solving," unpublished reflections, Georgetown University, 1987.

15. Vahid Alavian, personal communication, Israel, 2012.

16. Sharon Pickett, "Preparing for Practice," *ACResolution* 5, no. 1 (Fall 2005), 4.

Chapter 6

1. See Michelle LeBaron, *Bridging Cultural Conflicts: A New Approach for a Changing World* (San Francisco: Wiley, 2003); and Michelle LeBaron and Venashri Pillay, *Conflict across Cultures: A Unique Experience of Bridging Differences* (Boston: Intercultural Press, 2006) for more detail on cross-cultural conflict and cooperation. For those interested in

pursuing the topic in more depth, the Intercultural Communication Institute has summer trainings and an extensive online library: http://intercultural.org.

2. Brooks Peterson, *Cultural Intelligence: A Guide to Working with People from Other Cultures* (Yarmouth, ME: Intercultural Press, 2004).

3. Diana Suhardiman, personal communication, 2013.

4. William Ury, *Getting Past No: Negotiation with Difficult People* (New York: Bantam, 1991).

5. Rosenberg spearheaded a movement for nonviolent communication for education and training in how our communication can circumvent apparent threats to our needs and instead heal relationships. See Marshall B. Rosenberg, *Nonviolent Communication: A Language of Life* (Encinitas, CA: PuddleDancer Press, 1998; Marshall B. Rosenberg, *Speak Peace in a World of Conflict* (Encinitas, CA: PuddleDancer Press, 2005); and Marshall B. Rosenberg, *Living Nonviolent Communication: Practical Tools to Connect and Communicate Skillfully in Every Situation* (Boulder, CO: Sounds True, 2012) for more information.

6. Daniel Goleman, *Emotional Intelligence* (New York: Bantam Books, 1996).

7. Marshall B. Rosenberg recognizes these roots in his monograph, *Practical Spirituality: Reflections on the Spiritual Basis of Nonviolent Communication* (Encinitas, CA: Puddle-Dancer Press, 2004).

8. For more on the construct and practical meditations to help guide the seeker, see Ozer Bergman, *Where Earth and Heaven Kiss: A Guide to Rebbe Nachman's Path of Meditation* (Jerusalem: Breslov Research Institute, 2006).

9. The Book of Mormon echoes much of Christianity's balance of works and grace: "Yea, come unto Christ, and be perfected in him, and deny yourselves of all ungodliness; and if ye shall deny yourselves of all ungodliness, and love God with all your might, mind and strength, then is his grace sufficient for you, that by his grace ye may be perfect in Christ; and if by the grace of God ye are perfect in Christ, ye can in nowise deny the power of God" (Moroni 10:32, *Book of Mormon*).

10. Laurence-Khantipālo Mills, *Buddhism Explained* (Chiang Mai, Thailand: Silkworm Books, 1999), 1.

11. Walpola Rahula, in *What the Buddha Taught* (Grove Press, Kindle edition, 2007), echoing most English-speaking scholars and practitioners of Buddhism, calls "suffering" a "highly unsatisfactory and misleading" translation of *dukkha* (p. 16). He suggests that the actual meaning connotes "enormously wider senses . . . and includes deeper ideas such as 'imperfection', 'impermanence', 'emptiness', 'insubstantiality'" (p. 17).

12. Phra Paisan, personal communication, 2005; Mills, *Buddhism Explained*; Rahula, *What the Buddha Taught*.

13. Sulak Sivaraksa, *Conflict, Culture and Change: Engaged Buddhism in a Globalizing World* (Boston: Wisdom Publications, 2005), 3.

14. Again, the structure is fairly universal: "All things," Lao Tzu writes, "carry Yin and embrace Yang. Dynamic balance creates harmony." Lao Tzu, Chapter 42, in *The 81 Chapters of Tao Te Ching by Lao Tzu*, translated, explained, and commented by Stefan Stenudd, e-book. http://www.taoistic.com/taoteching-laotzu/taoteching-42.htm.

15. Again, I am aware of how much conflation there is in this paragraph, with an extreme simplification of exceedingly nuanced and elaborate theologies dating back centuries. For elucidation, see Gershom Scholem, *On the Kabbalah and Its Symbolism* (New York: Schocken Books, 1965); and any version of Rabbi Schneur Zalman of Liadi's (1745–1812) *The Tanya*. Rabbi Rami Shapiro has an accessible translation and commentary: Rami M. Shapiro and Rabbi Zalman M. Schachter-Shalomi, *Tanya, the Masterpiece of Hasidic Wisdom: Selections Annotated & Explained* (Woodstock, VT: SkyLight Paths

Pub., 2010); while Rabbi Yosef Wineberg's is more detailed and academic: Yosef Wineberg et al., *Lessons in Tanya (5 vols.) by Rabbi Schneur Zalman of Liadi* (Brooklyn, NY: Kehot Publication Society, 1998).

16. As the old adage goes, when we point at others, three fingers point back at us.

17. I am grateful to Dr. Shaiya Rothberg, in whose course on Kabbalah at the Conservative Yeshivah in Jerusalem I studied these concepts. He elaborated on the link between the individual and the divine and between the individual to the collective, suggesting that "the principle of evil comes from justice" and originates at the line between righteousness and self-righteousness. He also noted that an overabundance of love (the right side of the map) can be destructive as well. (Personal communications, July 19, 2004.)

18. Dr. Shaiya Rothberg, personal communication, November 17, 2004.

19. I am grateful to Sherzod Asadov of the Foreign Ministry of Uzbekistan, a country mired for years in difficult water negotiations with its upstream neighbors over dams and development. I used to use the word *unity*, which to me echoed spirituality, but in 2014 he offered *harmony* as more representative of the balance and protection of both self and other.

20. Dianne Hall, Yi Guo, and Robert A. Davis, "Developing a Value-Based Decision-Making Model for Inquiring Organizations," *Proceedings of the 36th Hawaii International Conference on System Sciences (HICSS), January 6–9, 2003, Big Island, HI* (IEEE Computer Society Press, 2003).

21. E. Spranger, *Types of Men: The Psychology and Ethics of Personality* (New York: Johnson, 1928/1966).

22. J. F. Courtney, "Decision Making and Knowledge Management in Inquiring Organizations: A New Decision-Making Paradigm for DSS," *Decision Support Systems Special Issue on Knowledge Management* 31 (2001): 17–38.

23. Richard Barrett Values Centre. http://www.valuescentre.com/about/richard-barrett/.

24. D. Shmueli, M. Elliott, and S. Kaufman, "Frame Changes and the Management of Intractable Conflicts," *Conflict Resolution Quarterly* 24, no. 2 (Winter 2006): 207–218.

25. Shmueli, Elliott, and Kaufman, "Frame Changes," 209.

26. Julia Doermann and Aaron T. Wolf, "Western Water Participant Workbook," *Sharing Water, Building Relations: Managing and Transforming Water Conflict in the US West* (Denver: U.S. Department of the Interior Bureau of Reclamation, 2012), http://www.transboundarywaters.orst.edu/research/US%20Western%20Water/Western%20Water%20Participant%20Workbook%202012.pdf.

27. Doermann and Wolf, "Western Water Participant Workbook," 111.

28. Doermann and Wolf, "Western Water Participant Workbook," 110.

29. Reproduced in Doermann and Wolf, "Western Water Participant Workbook."

30. Robert A. Heinlein, *Stranger in a Strange Land (Remembering Tomorrow)* (New York: Putnam, 1961), 253.

31. "Grok," Merriam-Webster.com (Merriam-Webster, n.d., accessed December 21, 2016).

32. The chronology of the relevant verses is vague in the text, and rabbis have interpreted the commitments made in Exodus 24:7 (ArtScroll Chumash) as coming before the Children of Israel have received the Torah (*Mekhilta d'Rabbi Shimon bar Yochai* 24:7).

33. Enzo Bianchi, "Listening," chapter 5 in *Lectio Divina: From God's Word to Our Lives* (Brewster, MA: Paraclete Press, 2015), n.p. (in digital version).

34. Pravrajika Virajaprana, "The Art of Listening" (Los Angeles: Vedanta Society of Southern California), https://vedanta.org/2013/monthly-readings/the-art-of-listening-part-1-2/.

35. Thich Nhat Hanh, *The Art of Communicating* (New York: HarperCollins Publishers, 2013).

36. Andrea S. Cohen, Leah Green, and Susan Partnow, *Practicing the Art of Compassionate Listening* (Indianola, WA: The Compassionate Listening Project, 2011).

37. Barbara Eve Breitman, "Holy Listening: Cultivating a Hearing Heart," in *Jewish Spiritual Direction: An Innovative Guide from Traditional and Contemporary Sources*, ed. Rabbi Howard Avruhm Addison and Barbara Eve Breitman (Woodstock, VT: Jewish Lights, 2006).

38. 1 Kings 3:9 (ArtScroll Chumash).

39. Cohen, Green, and Partnow, *Practicing the Art of Compassionate Listening*, 10.

40. Bianchi, *Lectio Divina*, n.p.

41. *Grok* may well be a more intuitive term, here, especially since Heinlein's Smith understands the concept of God as "one who *groks*" (see note 30).

42. Rabbi Ozer Bergman, personal communication (2004), and Bergman, *Where Earth and Heaven Kiss*, 18.

43. Bergman, *Where Earth and Heaven Kiss*.

44. Huston Smith, *The World's Religions: Our Great Wisdom Traditions* (San Francisco, CA: HarperSanFrancisco, 1991), 261.

45. Stephen R. Covey, *The 7 Habits of Highly Effective People* (New York: Free Press, 1989); Stephen R. Covey, *The 8th Habit: From Effectiveness to Greatness* (New York: Free Press, 2004).

46. Which actually seems to have originated around World War I, not with St. Francis of Assisi. See Friar J. Poulenc, OFM, "L'inspiration Moderne de la Priere 'Seigneru faites de moi un instrument de votre paix,'" *Archivum Franciscanum Historicum* 68 (1975), 450–453.

47. John A. McConnell, *Mindful Mediation: A Handbook for Buddhist Peacemakers* (Bangkok, Thailand: Buddhist Research Institute, 1995), 228.

48. Prof. Father José Galván, personal communication, 2013.

49. Charlotte Anderson, comp., *The Manual on Pranic Energy Healing Level I*, Pranic Energy Healing, 2012. http://www.pranicenergyhealing.net/wp-content/uploads/2012/08/FINAL-Revised-Manual-on-PEH-Lv-I-14-Aug-2012.pdf.

50. Paramahansa Yogananda, *Autobiography of a Yogi* (New York: The Philosophical Library, Inc., 1946, e-book).

51. Daniel Goleman, "The Social Brain," *More than Sound Podcast*, no. 93 (August 23, 2013), http://morethansound.net/2013/08/23/social-brain/#.V8hnKmUjpT4.

52. I Kings 19:12 (ArtScroll Chumash).

53. Ann Kline, "Chavurat Ruach (A Fellowship of Spirit): Community for Spiritual Direction," in *Jewish Spiritual Direction: An Innovative Guide from Traditional and Contemporary Sources*, ed. Rabbi Howard A. Addison and Barbara Eve Breitman (Nashville, TN: Jewish Lights, 2006).

54. Mirabai Bush, "Working with Mindfulness" webinar featuring George Kohlrieser, *More than Sound Podcast*, no. 94 (August 30, 2013), http://morethansound.net/?powerpress_pinw =7135-podcast.

55. Erica Ariel Fox and Marc Gafni, "Seeing with New Eyes: One Step toward the Field of the Future," *ACResolution* 5, no. 1 (Fall 2005), 22–25.

56. Gershon Winkler, *Magic of the Ordinary: Recovering the Shamanic in Judaism* (Berkeley, CA: North Atlantic Books, 2003), 193–194.

57. Smith, *The World's Religions*, 262.

58. From *Sefer Yetsira* 1:8 ("Book of Formation" [Second Mishnah]), quoted in Winkler, *Magic of the Ordinary*, 199. In the classic Mishnaic commentary *Pirkei Avot* (Ethics of the Fathers), Rabbi Shimon writes, "All my days have I grown up among the wise and I have not found anything better for a man than silence. Studying Torah is not the most important thing; rather fulfilling it. Whoever multiplies words causes sin" (Chap. 1 #17).

59. Yogananda, *Autobiography of a Yogi*, 243.

60. Sheikh Fara Gaye, personal communication, Vatican City, 2004.

61. Michelle Lebaron, personal communication, 2010.

62. For more information and training workshops and manuals, visit the Center for Non-violent Communications online at https://www.cnvc.org/trainingcal.

63. Swami Subodhananda, personal communication, 2013.

64. This entire process, and the skills that accompany it, were learned from Uzi Weingarten in his powerful and highly recommended distance-ed course, "Communicating with Compassion," offered online at http://uziteaches.com/.

Chapter 7

1. Daryl Fields, senior water resources specialist, World Bank, personal communication, 2016.

2. S. O. Wade, "Using Intentional, Values-Based Dialogue to Engage Complex Public Policy Conflicts," *Conflict Resolution Quarterly* 21 (2004), 364.

3. These stages build primarily on the work of Jay Rothman, who initially described his stages as ARI (Adversarial, Reflexive, and Integrative) in "Supplementing Tradition: A Theoretical and Practical Typology for International Conflict Management," *Negotiation Journal* 5, no. 3 (1989). When ARI became ARIA, adding "Action," Rothman's terminology also evolved to "Antagonism, Resonance, Invention, and Action." See Jay Rothman, *Resolving Identity-Based Conflicts in Nations, Organizations, and Communities* (San Francisco: Jossey-Bass, 1997). We retain the former terms, feeling they are more descriptive for our purposes.

4. Both the structure and application of the ARIA model are described eloquently in Rothman, *Resolving Identity-Based Conflicts*, and Jay Rothman, ed., *From Identity-Based Conflict to Identity-Based Cooperation: The ARIA Approach in Theory and Practice.* (New York: Springer, 2012).

5. See Steven E. Daniels and Gregg B. Walker, *The Collaborative Learning Approach* (Westport, CT: Praeger, 2001) for elucidation on collaborative learning.

6. Edy Kaufman, "Innovative Problem-Solving Workshops," in *Second Track/Citizens' Diplomacy: Concepts and Techniques for Conflict Transformation*, ed. John Davies and Edy Kaufman (Lanham, MD: Rowman & Littlefield, 2002), 171–247.

7. Phra Paisan Visalo, personal communication, 2005.

8. Tomas D. Andres, *Negotiating by Filipino Values* (Manila: Divine Word Publications, 1988), 33–36.

9. All quotes in this section are from Barbarah Miller and Vahid Alavian's summary of the process of consultation (personal communications and unpublished manuscript, n.d.), the latter of which in turn draws from classic sources and from John E. Kolstoe, *Consultation: A Universal Lamp of Guidance* (Oxford: G. Ronald, 1985).

10. Text from Peacemaker Ministries, http://peacemaker.net/about/first-visit-please-read-this/ (2014).

11. Ben Campbell Johnson, ed., *Sacred Space* (Atlanta, GA: Interfaith Community Institute, 2011), 65.

12. Ashad Sentongo and Andrea Bartoli, "Conflict Resolution under the *Ekika* System of the Baganda in Uganda," in *Integrating Traditional and Modern Conflict Resolution: Experiences from Selected Cases in Eastern and the Horn of Africa*, ed. Martha Mutisi and Kwesi Sansculotte-Greenidge, Africa Dialogue Monograph Series no. 2/2012 (Durban, South Africa: Accord Press, 2012).

13. Morihei Ueshiba and John Stevens, *The Art of Peace* (Boston: Shambhala, 2002), 92.

14. Jennifer Beer and Eileen Stief, *The Mediator's Handbook* (Gabriola Island, BC: New Society Publishers, 1997).

15. Elias Jabbour, *Sulha: Palestinian Traditional Peacemaking Process* (Montreat, NC: House of Hope Publications, 1993, 1996), 56.

16. Prof. Father José Galván, personal communication, 2013.

17. Dena Marshall, an extraordinary mediator based in Portland, Oregon, has written and presented on the transformative moment in mediation, including her experience with First Foods festivals (personal communication, 2013).

18. For more, see Michelle LeBaron, *Bridging Troubled Waters: Conflict Resolution from the Heart* (San Francisco: Jossey-Bass, 2002); and Michelle LeBaron, *Bridging Cultural Conflicts: A New Approach for a Changing World* (San Francisco: Wiley, 2003).

19. Vasudha Narayanan, personal communication, 2004.

20. Barbarah Miller, personal communication, 2012. Nili Sneh and John Tristan have an interesting article on using Japanese art of plant arranging to help facilitate dialogue: "Plant Material Arrangement in Therapy: An Innovative Method," n.d., unpublished.

21. Thanks to Aharon N. Varady, we know that this is actually from Gerald G. Jampolsky, *Love Is Letting Go of Fear* (Millbrae, CA: Celestial Arts, 1979), as paraphrased by Corinne Edwards, cited in Aharon Varady, "Tracking Down the Author of the Popular Quote, 'Forgiveness Means Giving Up All Hope for a Better Past.'" *Omphalos* (April 19, 2016). http://aharon.varady.net/omphalos/2016/04/first-said-forgiveness-giving-hope-better-past.

22. Sheikh Fara Gaye, personal communication, 2004.

23. Ken Sande, *The Peacemaker: A Biblical Guide to Resolving Personal Conflict*, 3rd ed. (Grand Rapids, MI: Baker Books, 2003), 209.

24. Ancient Huna.com, "What Is Huna; Basic Huna; Ho'oponopono," http://www.ancienthuna.com/ho-oponopono.htm.

25. Thomas J. Butler, "Blood Feuds and Traditional Forms of Peacebuilding in the Old Yugoslavia," *Bulletin of the Boston Theological Institute* 5.1 (Fall 2005): 16–18.

26. Fred Luskin, *Forgive for Good, A Proven Prescription for Health and Happiness* (New York: Harper Collins, 2002).

27. Raymond G. Helmick, S. J. Petersen, and Rodney L. Petersen, eds., *Forgiveness and Reconciliation: Religion, Public Policy, and Conflict Transformation* (Philadelphia & London: Templeton Foundation Press, 2001).

28. Roy Bear Chief, Allan E. Barsky, and David Este, "Theft by a Cree Woman: Victim–Offender Mediation versus Healing Circle," Chapter 7 in *Interprofessional Practice with Diverse Populations: Cases in Point*, ed. E. Geva, A. Barsky, and F. Westernoff (Westport, CT: Auburn House, 2000).

29. From Visalo, personal communication, 2005, and from the Ven. Dhammawiranatha Nayaka Mahathera, http://www.buddhayana.nl.

30. Albert Lincoln, personal communication, January 2013.

31. Barbarah Miller, personal communication, January 2013.

32. "Reconciliation in Judaism, Islam and Christianity," *Newsletter of The Interfaith Encounter Association* (November 11, 2003).

33. That's not to say that discussions could not be contentious. A quote attributed to many, but probably originating with Wallace Stanley Sayre from Columbia University, sums up the tenor of academic decision making: "Academic politics is the most vicious and bitter form of politics, because the stakes are so low," from "Politics and People," by Alan L. Otten, *Wall Street Journal* (1973, December 20), 14. Having said that, I must admit that we have a really collegial faculty.

34. For more information, see M. Shane Smith, "Single Text Negotiation." In *Beyond Intractability*, ed. Guy Burgess and Heidi Burgess (Boulder: Conflict Information Consortium, University of Colorado, July 2005). http://www.beyondintractability.org/essay/single-text-negotiation.

35. Rabbi Zalman Schachter-Shalomi, with Joel Segel, *Jewish with Feeling: A Guide to Meaningful Jewish Practice* (New York: Riverhead Books, 2005), 178.

36. Ueshiba and Stevens, *Art of Peace*, 69.

37. Edy Kaumann, personal communication, 2013.

38. Co-Intelligence Institute, "Listening Circles," http://www.co-intelligence.org/P-listeningcircles.html.

39. Ibn Yusuf, personal communication, 2005.

40. Paramahansa Yogananda, *Autobiography of a Yogi* (New York: The Philosophical Library, Inc., 1946, e-book).

41. Subbappa Ribeiro, Michele Ribeiro, and Glen Hearns, personal communication, 2016.

42. Ueshiba and Stevens, *The Art of Peace*, 43.

43. Stephanie Hixon and Thomas Porter, *Engage Conflict Well*, version 1.4 (2011). http://justpeaceumc.org/wp-content/uploads/2014/08/Engage-Conflict-Well.pdf.

Chapter 8

1. For the best thinking along these lines, see C. O. Scharmer, *Theory U* (Cambridge, MA: SoL Press, 2004); and Peter Senge et al., *Presence: Exploring Profound Change in People, Organizations, and Society* (New York: Crown, 2004).

2. Rabbi Zalman Schachter-Shalomi, with Joel Segel, *Jewish with Feeling: A Guide to Meaningful Jewish Practice* (New York: Riverhead Books, 2005), 178.

Bibliography

'Abdu'l-Bahá. *The Promulgation of Universal Peace: Talks Delivered by 'Abdu'l-Bahá during His Visit to the United States and Canada in 1912.* Compiled by Howard MacNutt, available at: http://www.bahai.org/library/authoritative-texts/abdul-baha/promulgation-universal-peace/#r=pup_en-title.

Abou El Fadl, Khaled. *Islam and the Challenge of Democracy.* Princeton, NJ: Princeton University Press, 2004.

al-Jerrahi, Sheikh Ragip Robert Frager. *Introduction to Essential Sufism,* ed. James Fadiman and Robert Frager. San Francisco: HarperSanFrancisco, 1999.

Ancient Huna.com. "What Is Huna; Basic Huna; Ho'oponopono." http://www.ancient huna.com/ho-oponopono.htm.

Anderson, Charlotte, comp. *The Manual on Pranic Energy Healing Level I.* Pranic Energy Healing, 2012. http://www.pranicenergyhealing.net/wp-content/uploads/2012/08/FINAL-Revised-Manual-on-PEH-Lv-I-14-Aug-2012.pdf.

Andres, Tomas D. *Negotiating by Filipino Values.* Manila: Divine Word Publications, 1988.

Ariyadhamma, Ven. Mahathera Nauyane. "Anapana Sati: Meditation on Breathing" (1994), in *A Theravada Library,* at Access to Insight, 2005. Available at: http://www.accesstoin sight.org/lib/authors/ariyadhamma/bl115.html.

Baal Shem Tov, as quoted in "Rabbi Israel Baal Shem Tov (1698–1760), Founder of the Chassidic Movement." Chabad.org. http://www.chabad.org/generic_cdo/aid/388609/jew ish/The-Baal-Shem-Tov.htm?gclid=CNqG3-PG-dACFUGTfgodvp8Lig.

Bahá'í Administration. A selection of letters and messages addressed to the Bahá'ís of the United States and Canada, written between January 1922 and July 1932, p. 45, available at: http://www.bahai.org/library/authoritative-texts/shoghi-effendi/bahai-administration/.

Barker, Eileen. "What the BLEEP Does Spirituality Have to Do with Conflict Resolution?" *ACResolution* 5, no. 1 (Fall 2005): 10–11.

Barrett, Richard. Barrett Values Centre. http://www.valuescentre.com/about/richard-barrett/.

Barthel, Trip. "Unity and Diversity in Conflict Resolution." *ACResolution* 5, no. 1 (Fall 2005): 32.

Bear Chief, Roy, Allan Barsky, and David Este. "Theft by a Cree Woman: Victim–Offender Mediation versus Healing Circle." In *Interprofessional Practice with Diverse Populations: Cases in Point,* ed. Esther Geva, Allan Barsky, and Fern Westernoff. Westport, CT: Auburn House, 2000. 127–146.

Beer, Jennifer E., and Eileen Stief. *The Mediator's Handbook.* Developed by the (Quaker) Friends Conflict Resolution Programs. Gabriola Island, BC: New Society Publishers, 1997.

ben Asher, R. Bachya. *Midrash Rabbeinu Bachya,* first published in 1492; currently available in English and Hebrew as *Rabbeinu Bachya: Commentary on the Torah.* New York: Judaica Press, 1998, seven volumes.

Benedict XVI. "Lecture of the Holy Father: Faith, Reason and the University Memories and Reflections." *Libreria Editrice Vaticana* (September 12, 2006). Accessed November 26, 2016, http://w2.vatican.va/content/benedict-xvi/en/speeches/2006/september/documents/hf_ben-xvi_spe_20060912_university-regensburg.html.

Berg, Leon. "The Power of Listening—An Ancient Practice for Our Future: Leon Berg at TEDxRedondoBeach." https://www.youtube.com/watch?v=6iDMuB6NjNA&feature=youtu.be.

Bergman, Ozer. *Where Earth and Heaven Kiss: A Guide to Rebbe Nachman's Path of Meditation.* Jerusalem: Breslov Research Institute, 2006.

Bhikkhu, Buddhadā. *Mindfulness with Breathing: A Manual for Serious Beginners.* Trans. Santikaro Bhikkhu. Bangkok: The Dhamma Study & Practice Group, with help from Evolution/Liberation, 1988. http://www.dhammatalks.net/Books3/Bhikkhu_Buddhadasa_Anapanasati_Mindfulness_with_Breathing.htm.

Bianchi, Enzo. "Listening." Chapter 5 in *Lectio Divina: From God's Word to Our Lives.* Brewster, MA: Paraclete Press, 2015.

Bopp, Julie, Michael Bopp, Lee Brown, and Phil Lane, Jr. *Sacred Tree: Reflections on Native American Spirituality.* Twin Lakes, WI: Lotus Press, 1984.

Bowling, Daniel. "Who Am I as a Mediator? Mindfulness, Reflection and Presence." *ACResolution* 5, no. 1 (Fall 2005): 12–15.

Bowling, Daniel, and David A. Hoffman. *Bringing Peace into the Room: How the Personal Qualities of the Mediator Impact the Process of Conflict Resolution.* San Francisco: Jossey-Bass, 2003.

Brady, Mark, ed. *The Wisdom of Listening.* Somerville, MA: Wisdom Publications, 2003.

Breitman, Barbara Eve. "Holy Listening: Cultivating a Hearing Heart." In *Jewish Spiritual Direction: An Innovative Guide from Traditional and Contemporary Sources,* ed. Rabbi Howard Avruhm Addison and Barbara Eve Breitman. Woodstock, VT: Jewish Lights, 2006.

Burgess, Heidi. "Transformative Mediation: A Summary." Boulder, CO: University of Colorado Conflict Research Consortium, 1997. http://www.colorado.edu/conflict/transform/tmall.htm. Last accessed December 18, 2016.

Burns, Bill. "The Four Senses of Scripture." *Is My Phylactery Showing?* (blog). May 16, 2007. http://theocoid.blogspot.com/2007/05/four-senses-of-scripture.html.

Bush, Mirabai. "Working with Mindfulness" webinar featuring George Kohlrieser. *More than Sound Podcast,* no. 94 (August 30, 2013). http://morethansound.net/?powerpress_pinw=7135-podcast.

Butler, Thomas J. "Blood Feuds and Traditional Forms of Peacebuilding in the Old Yugoslavia." *Bulletin of the Boston Theological Institute* 5.1 (Fall 2005): 16–18.

Campbell, Joseph. *The Mythic Image.* Princeton, NJ: Princeton University Press, 1974.

Carrera, J. *Inside the Yoga Sutras: A Comprehensive Sourcebook for the Study and Practice of Patanjali's Yoga Sutras.* Buckingham, VA: Integral Yoga Publications, 2006.

Center for Nonviolent Communication. Workshops and training schedule. 2016. https://www.cnvc.org/trainingcal.

Cloke, Kenneth. *The Crossroads of Conflict: A Journey into the Heart of Dispute Resolution.* Calgary, AB: Janis, 2006.

Cloke, Kenneth. "Why Every Conflict Breaks Your Heart: Conflict as a Spiritual Crisis." *ACResolution* 5, no. 1 (Fall 2005): 16–21.

Co-Intelligence Institute, "Listening Circles," http://www.co-intelligence.org/P-listeningcircles.html.

Cohen, Andrea S., Leah Green, and Susan Partnow. *Practicing the Art of Compassionate Listening*. Indianola, WA: The Compassionate Listening Project, 2011.

Courtney, J. F. "Decision Making and Knowledge Management in Inquiring Organizations: A New Decision-Making Paradigm for DSS," *Decision Support Systems Special Issue on Knowledge Management* 31 (2001): 17–38.

Covey, Stephen R. *The 7 Habits of Highly Effective People*. New York: Free Press, 1989.

Covey, Stephen R. *The 8th Habit: From Effectiveness to Greatness*. New York: Free Press, 2004.

Daniels, Steven E., and Gregg B. Walker. *The Collaborative Learning Approach*. Westport, CT: Praeger, 2001.

Delli Priscoli, Jerome. "Christology and Faith Experience of Dispute Resolution and Collaborative Problem Solving." Unpublished reflections, Georgetown University, 1987.

De Mello, Anthony. *Sadhana, a Way to God: Christian Exercises in Eastern Form*. New York, NY: Doubleday, 1978.

Doermann, Julia, and Aaron T. Wolf. *Sharing Water, Building Relations: Managing and Transforming Water Conflict in the US West*. Denver: U.S. Department of the Interior Bureau of Reclamation, 2012. http://www.transboundarywaters.orst.edu/research/US%20 Western%20Water/Western%20Water%20Participant%20Workbook%202012.pdf.

Ferguson, Craig. "Does This Need to Be Said?" Online video clip. Comedy Central, October 7, 2011. http://www.cc.com/video-clips/2499vl/stand-up-craig-ferguson--uncensored ---does-this-need-to-be-said-.

Fischer, Frank. *Citizens, Experts, and the Environment: The Politics of Local Knowledge*. Durham, NC: Duke UP, 2000.

Fisher, Tom. "Beginner's Mind: Cultivating Mediator Mindfulness." *ACResolution* 5, no. 1 (Fall 2005): 28–29.

Four Worlds International Institute. http://www.fwii.net.

Fox, Erica Ariel. *Winning from Within: A Breakthrough Method for Leading, Living, and Lasting Change*. New York: Harper Business, 2013.

Fox, Erica Ariel, and Marc Gafni. "Seeing with New Eyes: One Step toward the Field of the Future." *ACResolution* 5, no. 1 (Fall 2005): 22–25.

Goleman, Daniel. *Emotional Intelligence*. New York: Bantam Books, 1996.

Goleman, Daniel. "The Social Brain." *More than Sound Podcast*, no. 93 (August 23, 2013). http://morethansound.net/2013/08/23/social-brain/#.V8hnKmUjpT4.

Gopin, Marc. *Between Eden and Armageddon: The Future of World Religions, Violence, and Peacemaking*. Oxford: Oxford University Press, 2000.

Gopin, Marc. *Healing the Heart of Conflict: Eight Crucial Steps to Making Peace with Yourself and Others*. Kutztown, PA: Rodale Books, 2004.

Green, Arthur. *Ehyeh: A Kabbalah for Tomorrow*. Nashville, TN: Jewish Lights Publishing, 2004.

Greisman, Nechoma. "Noach: Looking at Yourself Through Others," ed. Rabbi Moshe Miller. Chabad.org. http://www.chabad.org/library/article_cdo/aid/97527/jewish /Noach-Looking-at-Yourself-Through-Others.htm.

Hall, Dianne, Yi Guo, and Robert A. Davis. "Developing a Value-Based Decision-Making Model for Inquiring Organizations." *Proceedings of the 36th Hawaii International Conference on System Sciences, January 6–9, 2003, Big Island, HI*. IEEE Computer Society Press, 2003.

Hall, Edward T. *Beyond Culture*. New York: Anchor Books, 1976.

Halpern, Manfred. *Transforming the Personal, Political, Historical and Sacred in Theory and Practice*. Scranton, PA: University of Scranton Press, 2009.

Haònh, Nhâìt, and Annabel Laity. *The Sutra on the Full Awareness of Breathing: With Commentary by Thich Nhat Hanh.* Berkeley: Parallax Press, 1988.

Harvard Negotiation Insight Initiative. "Launching Document." Unpublished manuscript, 2003. http://www.pon.harvard.edu/tag/harvard-negotiation-institute/.

Heinlein, Robert A. *Stranger in a Strange Land (Remembering Tomorrow).* New York: Putnam, 1961.

Helmick, Raymond G., S. J. Petersen, and Rodney L. Petersen, eds. *Forgiveness and Reconciliation: Religion, Public Policy, and Conflict Transformation.* Philadelphia & London: Templeton Foundation Press, 2001.

Hixon, Stephanie, and Thomas Porter. *Engage Conflict Well.* Version 1.4. 2011. http://just peaceumc.org/wp-content/uploads/2014/08/Engage-Conflict-Well.pdf.

Hwoschinsky, Carol. "Listening to the Heart." *Alternatives* 25 (Spring 2003).

Interfaith Encounter Association. "Reconciliation in Judaism, Islam and Christianity." *Newsletter of the Interfaith Encounter Association* (November, 11 2003). http://interfaith-en counter.org/.

Irani, George. "Islamic Mediation Techniques for Middle East Conflicts." *Middle East Review of International Affairs (MERIA) Journal* 3, no. 2 (June 1999): n.p.

Jabbour, Elias. *Sulha: Palestinian Traditional Peacemaking Process.* Montreat, NC: House of Hope Publications, 1993, 1996.

Jampolsky, Gerald G. *Love Is Letting Go of Fear.* Millbrae, CA: Celestial Arts, 1979.

Jankowski, Peter J. "Postmodern Spirituality: Implications for Promoting Change." *Counseling and Values* 47, no. 1 (October 2002): 69–79.

Jarus, Owen. "Angkor Wat: History of Ancient Temple." *LiveScience* (October 8, 2014). http://www.livescience.com/23841-angkor-wat.html.

Johnson, Ben Campbell, ed. *Sacred Space.* Atlanta, GA: Interfaith Community Institute, 2011.

Kabbalah Online. "Lessons from the Dreidel." Chabad.org. Accessed December 8, 2016, http://www.chabad.org/kabbalah/article_cdo/aid/1693257/jewish/Lessons-from -the-Dreidel.htm.

Karr, Don. "The Study of Christian Cabala in English." *Hermetic Kabbalah.* Updated November 7, 2016. http://www.digital-brilliance.com/contributed/Karr/Biblios/ccinea.pdf.

Kaufman, Edy. "Innovative Problem-Solving Workshops." In *Second Track/Citizens' Diplomacy: Concepts and Techniques for Conflict Transformation,* ed. John Davies and Edy Kaufman. Lanham, MD: Rowman & Littlefield, 2002. 171–247.

Keshavjee, Mohamed M. *Islam, Sharia & Alternative Dispute Resolution.* London: I. B. Tauris. 2013.

Kline, Ann. "Chavurat Ruach (A Fellowship of Spirit): Community for Spiritual Direction." In *Jewish Spiritual Direction: An Innovative Guide from Traditional and Contemporary Sources,* ed. Rabbi Howard A. Addison and Barbara Eve Breitman. Nashville, TN: Jewish Lights, 2006.

Kolstoe, John E. *Consultation: A Universal Lamp of Guidance.* Oxford: G. Ronald, 1985.

Lao Tzu. Chapter 42, in *The 81 Chapters of Tao Te Ching by Lao Tzu,* translated, explained, and commented by Stefan Stenudd. http://www.taoistic.com/taoteching-laotzu/taote ching-42.htm

LeBaron, Michelle. *Bridging Cultural Conflicts: A New Approach for a Changing World.* San Francisco: Wiley, 2003.

LeBaron, Michelle. *Bridging Troubled Waters: Conflict Resolution from the Heart.* San Francisco: Jossey-Bass, 2002.

LeBaron, Michelle, and Venashri Pillay. *Conflict across Cultures: A Unique Experience of Bridging Differences.* Boston: Intercultural Press, 2006.

Lederach, John Paul. *Building Peace: Sustainable Reconciliation in Divided Societies.* Washington, DC: U.S. Institute of Peace, 1997.

Lindahl, Kay. *The Sacred Art of Listening.* Woodstock, VT: Skylight Paths Publishing, 2002. Available online at http://www.sacredlistening.com/tlc_listening101.htm.

Luskin, Fred. *Forgive for Good, A Proven Prescription for Health and Happiness.* New York: Harper Collins, 2002.

Luskin, Frederic. "Transformative Practices for Integrating Mind–Body Spirit." *The Journal of Alternative and Complementary Medicine* 10 (Supplement 1, 2004): S15–23.

MacAusland, Steve. As quoted in Anonymous. "Massachusetts Episcopal Diocese Bases Reorganization on Watersheds." *Earthkeeping News* 5, no. 6 (September/October 1996): 1–2.

Mannikka, Eleanor. *Angkor: Celestial Temples of the Khmer Empire.* New York: Abbeville Press, 2002.

Martin, David. "The Religious and the Secular: Pressure Points and Alignments." Keynote address. Forum 2000, Prague, October 8, 2007.

Maslow, A. H. "A Theory of Human Motivation." *Psychological Review* 50 (1943): 370–396.

Matt, Daniel C. *The Essential Kabbalah: The Heart of Jewish Mysticism.* Edison, NJ: Castle Books, 1997.

McConnell, John A. *Mindful Mediation: A Handbook for Buddhist Peacemakers.* Bangkok: Buddhist Research Institute, 1995.

McKay, David O. *Conference Reports* (April 1967): 85, cited in Philip G. McLemore, "Mormon Mantras: A Journey of Spiritual Transformation." *Sunstone Magazine* (April 2006): 20–31.

McLemore, Philip G. "Mormon Mantras: A Journey of Spiritual Transformation." *Sunstone Magazine* (April 2006): 20–31.

Mekhilta de-Rabbi Shimon bar Yochai, translated and explicated by W. David Nelson. Philadelphia: The Jewish Publication Society, 2006.

Mills, Laurence Khantipālo. *Buddhism Explained.* Chiang Mai, Thailand: Silkworm Books, 1999.

Mottola, Anthony, trans. *The Spiritual Exercises of Saint Ignatius.* New York: Bantam, 1964.

Muhammedinur.com. "Shariat-Tarikat-Marifat-Hakikat." http://www.muhammedinur.com/En/islam/shariat-tarikat-marifat-hakikat.html. Accessed December 8, 2016.

Myss, Caroline. *Anatomy of the Spirit: The Seven Stages of Power and Healing.* New York: Three Rivers Press, 1996.

Nepo, Mark. *Seven Thousand Ways to Listen.* New York: Atria Paperback, 2012.

Nhat Hanh, Thich. *The Art of Communicating.* New York: HarperCollins Publishers, 2013.

Nhat Hanh, Thich. *Transformation & Healing: Sutra on the Four Establishments of Mindfulness.* Berkeley: Parallax Press, 1990.

Nichols, Michael P. *The Lost Art of Listening: How Learning to Listen Can Improve Relationships.* New York: The Guilford Press, 1995.

O'Connor, David. "The Design of Self-Supporting Dispute Resolution Programs." *Negotiation Journal* 8:2 (April 1992).

O'Connor, T. P., J. Duncan, and F. Quillard. "Criminology and Religion: The Shape of an Authentic Dialogue." *The Journal of Criminology & Public Policy* 5, no. 3 (2006): 559–570.

Otten, Alan L. "Politics and People," *Wall Street Journal,* December 20, 1973, 14.

Peacemaker Ministries. 2014. http://peacemaker.net/about/first-visit-please-read-this/.

Peterson, Brooks. 2004. *Cultural Intelligence: A Guide to Working with People from Other Cultures.* Yarmouth, ME: Intercultural Press.

Pickett, Sharon. "Preparing for Practice." *ACResolution* 5, no. 1 (Fall 2005): 4.

Poulenc, Friar J., OFM, "L'inspiration Moderne de la Priere 'Seigneru Faites de Moi un Instrument de Votre Paix.'" *Archivum Franciscanum Historicum* 68 (1975): 450–453.

Program in Water Conflict Management and Transformation (PWCMT), College of Earth, Ocean, and Atmospheric Sciences, Oregon State University. http://www.transbound arywaters.orst.edu.

Rahula, Walpola. *What the Buddha Taught*. Kindle edition. New York: Grove Press, 2007.

Riskin, Leonard L. "The Contemplative Lawyer: On the Potential Contributions of Mindfulness Meditation to Law Students, Lawyers, and Their Clients." *Harvard Negotiation Law Review* 7, no. 1 (Spring 2002): 1–67.

Riskin, Leonard L. "Mindfulness: Foundational Training for Dispute Resolution." *Journal of Legal Education* 4, no. 1 (March 2004): 79–90.

Rodgers, Scott. *The Mindful Mediator, Embracing the Uncertainty of Conflict*. http://themind fulmediator.com/about.html.

Rosenberg, Marshall B. *Living Nonviolent Communication: Practical Tools to Connect and Communicate Skillfully in Every Situation*. Boulder, CO: Sounds True, 2012.

Rosenberg, Marshall B. *Nonviolent Communication: A Language of Life*. Encinitas, CA: PuddleDancer Press, 1998.

Rosenberg, Marshall B. *Nonviolent Communication: A Language of Life*. 2nd ed. Encinitas, CA: Puddlejumper Press, 2003.

Rosenberg, Marshall B. *Practical Spirituality: Reflections on the Spiritual Basis of Nonviolent Communication*. Encinitas, CA: PuddleDancer Press, 2004.

Rosenberg, Marshall B. *Speak Peace in a World of Conflict*. Encinitas, CA: PuddleDancer Press, 2005.

Rothman, Jay, ed. *From Identity-Based Conflict to Identity-Based Cooperation: The ARIA Approach in Theory and Practice*. New York: Springer, 2012.

Rothman, Jay. *Resolving Identity-Based Conflicts in Nations, Organizations, and Communities*. San Francisco: Jossey-Bass, 1997.

Rothman, Jay. "Supplementing Tradition: A Theoretical and Practical Typology for International Conflict Management." *Negotiation Journal* 5, no. 3 (1989).

Ruiz, Don Miguel. *The Four Agreements: A Practical Guide to Personal Freedom*. San Rafael, CA: Amber-Allen Publishing, 1997.

Sande, Ken. *The Peacemaker: A Biblical Guide to Resolving Personal Conflict*. 3rd ed. Grand Rapids, MI: Baker Books, 2003.

Sayre, Wallace Stanley. Quoted in Alan L. Otten, "Politics and People." *Wall Street Journal*, December 20, 1973, 14.

Schachter-Shalomi, Rabbi Zalman, with Joel Segel. *Jewish with Feeling: A Guide to Meaningful Jewish Practice*. New York: Riverhead Books, 2005.

Schall, James V. *The Regensburg Lecture*. South Bend, IN: St. Augustine's Press, 2007.

Scharmer, C. O. *Theory U*. Cambridge, MA: SoL Press, 2004.

Scharmer, C. Otto. *Theory U: Leading from the Future as It Emerges: The Social Technology of Presencing*. Cambridge, MA: Society for Organizational Learning, 2007.

Scherman, R. Nosson, ed. *The Stone Edition Chumash*. New York: Mesorah Publications, 1993. Revised, 2001.

Scholem, Gershom. *On the Kabbalah and Its Symbolism*. New York: Schocken Books, 1965.

Schronck-Shenk, Carolyn, ed. *Mediation and Facilitation Training Manual*. 4th ed. Akron, PA: Mennonite Conciliation Service, 2000.

Schwartz, Arthur J. "The Nature of Spiritual Transformation: A Review of the Literature."

Unpublished manuscript, fall 2000. Available at: http://www.metanexus.net/archive/spiritualtransformationresearch/research/pdf/STSRP-LiteratureReview2-7.PDF.

Senge, Peter, C. Otto Scharmer, Joseph Jaworski, and Betty Sue Flowers. *Presence: Exploring Profound Change in People, Organizations, and Society.* New York: Crown, 2004.

Sentongo, Ashad, and Andrea Bartoli. "Conflict Resolution under the *Ekika* System of the Baganda in Uganda." In *Integrating Traditional and Modern Conflict Resolution: Experiences from Selected Cases in Eastern and the Horn of Africa,* ed. Martha Mutisi and Kwesi Sansculotte-Greenidge. Africa Dialogue Monograph Series no. 2/2012. Durban, South Africa: Accord Press, 2012.

Shafir, Rebecca Z. *The Zen of Listening: Mindful Communication in the Age of Distraction.* Wheaton, IL: Quest Books, 2000.

Shapiro, Rami M., and Rabbi Zalman M. Schachter-Shalomi. *Tanya, the Masterpiece of Hasidic Wisdom: Selections Annotated & Explained.* Woodstock, VT: SkyLight Paths Pub., 2010.

Shmueli, D., M. Elliott, and S. Kaufman. "Frame Changes and the Management of Intractable Conflicts." *Conflict Resolution Quarterly* 24, no. 2 (Winter 2006): 207–218.

Singer, Isidore, ed. "Enumeration and English Translation." In *The Jewish Encyclopedia.* New York: Funk & Wagnalls, 1904.

Sivaraksa, Sulak. *Conflict, Culture and Change: Engaged Buddhism in a Globalizing World.* Boston: Wisdom Publications, 2005.

Smith, Daniel L. "The Rewards of Allah." *Journal of Peace Research* 26, no. 4 (1989): 385–398.

Smith, Huston. *Forgotten Truth: The Common Vision of the World's Religions.* New York: HarperCollins, 1976.

Smith, Huston. *The World's Religions: Our Great Wisdom Traditions.* San Francisco, CA: HarperSanFrancisco, 1991 (revised and updated ed. of *The Religions of Man,* 1958).

Smith, M. Shane. "Single Text Negotiation." In *Beyond Intractability,* ed. Guy Burgess and Heidi Burgess. Boulder: Conflict Information Consortium, University of Colorado, July 2005. http://www.beyondintractability.org/essay/single-text-negotiation.

Spranger, E. *Types of Men: The Psychology and Ethics of Personality.* New York: Johnson, 1928/1966.

Tarabeih, H., D. Shmueli, and R. Khamaisi. "Towards the Implementation of Sulha as a Cultural Peacemaking Method for Managing and Resolving Environmental Conflicts Among Arab Palestinians in Israel." *Journal of Peacebuilding and Development* 5, no. 1(2009): 50–64.

Swami Tejomayananda. *Hindu Culture: An Introduction.* Mumbai: Central Chinmaya Mission Trust, 1993.

Ueshiba, Morihei, and John Stevens. *The Art of Peace.* Boston: Shambhala, 2002.

Umbreit, Mark. "Mindfulness, Deep Listening and Stories: The Spiritual Core of Peacemaking." *ACResolution* 5, no. 1 (Fall 2005): 26–27.

United States Catholic Conference, Inc. *English Translation of the Catechism of the Catholic Church.* 1997. http://www.catholicculture.org/culture/library/catechism/. Accessed August 11, 2015.

Ury, William. *Getting Past No: Negotiation with Difficult People.* New York: Bantam, 1991.

Varady, Aharon. "'Tracking Down the Author of the Popular Quote, 'Forgiveness Means Giving Up All Hope for a Better Past.'" *Omphalos* (April 19, 2016). http://aharon.varady.net/omphalos/2016/04/first-said-forgiveness-giving-hope-better-past.

Villoldo, Alberto. *The Four Insights: Wisdom, Power, and Grace of the Earthkeepers.* Carlsbad, CA: Hay House, 2006.

Virajaprana, Pravrajika. "The Art of Listening." Los Angeles: Vedanta Society of Southern California. https://vedanta.org/2013/monthly-readings/the-art-of-listening-part-1-2/.

Vivekananda, Swami. *The Complete Works of Swami Vivekananda, Volume 7, Conversations and Dialogues.* 1907 (original publication date). Available on Wikisource: https://en.wikisource.org/w/index.php?title=The_Complete_Works_of_Swami_Vivekananda/Volume_7/Conversations_And_Dialogues&oldid=4900933 (accessed December 16, 2016).

Wade, S. O. "Using Intentional, Values-Based Dialogue to Engage Complex Public Policy Conflicts." *Conflict Resolution Quarterly* 21 (2004): 361–379. doi:10.1002/crq.67.

Weingarten, Uzi. "Communicating with Compassion" course notes. Online class taught by Bernard Uzi Weingarten, 2003. Course now offered at http://uziteaches.com/.

Wilber, Ken. *A Theory of Everything: An Integral Vision for Business, Politics, Science, and Spirituality.* Boston: Shambhala, 2000.

Wineberg, Yosef, Levi Wineberg, Uri Kaploun, and Sholom Wineberg. *Lessons in Tanya (5 vols.) by Rabbi Schneur Zalman of Liadi.* Brooklyn, NY: Kehot Publication Society, 1998.

Winkler, Gershon. *Magic of the Ordinary: Recovering the Shamanic in Judaism.* Berkeley: North Atlantic Books, 2003.

Wolf, A. "Indigenous Approaches to Water Conflict Negotiations and Implications for International Waters." *International Negotiation: A Journal of Theory and Practice 5*, no. 2 (December 2000): 357–373.

Yogananda, Paramahansa. *Autobiography of a Yogi.* New York: The Philosophical Library, Inc., 1946, e-book.

Zalman, Shneur, and Rami M. Shapiro. *Tanya, the Masterpiece of Hasidic Wisdom: Selections Annotated & Explained.* Woodstock, VT: SkyLight Paths Publishing, 2010.

Zollo, Paul. *Songwriters on Songwriting.* Boston: Da Capo Press, 2003.

Index

Note: Page numbers followed by the letter b, f, or t indicate boxes, figures, or tables respectively.